INDEPENDENT
ON SUNDAY

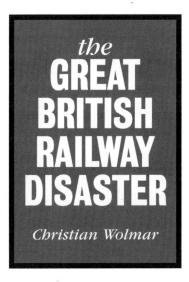

the
GREAT
BRITISH
RAILWAY
DISASTER

Christian Wolmar

D0490014

1.00

25.4

ON SUNDAY

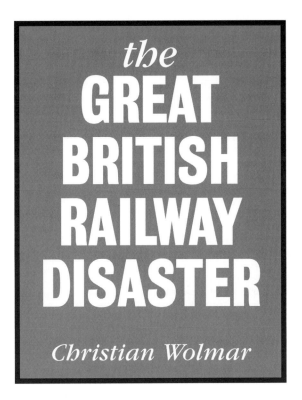

the
GREAT BRITISH RAILWAY DISASTER

Christian Wolmar

IAN ALLAN
Publishing

Acknowledgements

When the *Independent on Sunday* began the 'Mad' railway column in January 1995, the editors expected that it would run for a few weeks and then, like most such series, run out of steam. Instead, like Topsy, it grew and grew, because the letters kept rolling in. Indeed, this book has only been made possible by the hundreds of letters I have received from people about their experiences on the railways and I thank them all, even if their letters have not been used. I am also grateful to the many people in the railway industry, who would not thank me for naming them, who have helped me with items and even occasionally contributed them.

I would also like to thank Ian Jack, the former editor of the *Independent on Sunday* who had the idea for the column and indeed wrote the first one and Colin Wheeler, of the *Independent*, who drew the cartoons in this book. Peter Wilby, the current editor, and Mike McCarthy, the news editor, have also been very supportive of the project and I am grateful for their encouragement. Peter Waller at Ian Allan immediately understood what the project was about and has been very encouraging. Thanks, too, are due to the students Teilo Vellacott and Rosa Prince who actually wrote some of the items. And, of course, none of this would be possible without the support of Scarlett, who puts up with me for reasons known only to her, and my children, Molly, Pascoe and Misha, who inspire everything I do.

Christian Wolmar, February 1996

Credits

All photographs come from the Ian Allan Library with the following exceptions: p8 (Leeds City station 18 May 1967) Dr L. A. Nixon; p13 (Crewe station south end 6 February 1974) Philip D. Hawkins; p21 Esso; p25 (A Class 37 receives attention at Dingwall) C. J. M. Lofthus; p28 (pupils at Brynteg Comprehen-sive restore an ex-Taff Vale coach) Teg Jones; p34 (peeling sign at Claydon 10 May 1978) Kevin Lane; p41 (A 'Western' heads out of Paddington in November 1976) R. Carvell; p45 (Evidence of vandalism) Brian Morrison; p47 (Bolton station 19 March 1977) Kevin Lane; p49 (Class 08 shunter at Newcastle 11 March 1988) Ian S. Carr; p58 (Class 50 No 50043 at Basingstoke on 22 November 1987) Brian Perryman; p61 M. Dunnett; p63 (Edinburgh Waverley's new station hostess office on 8 September 1983) Colin Boocock; p66 (Etchingham station) J. Scrace; p72 (Shunting wagons at Stowmarket) W. S. Garth; p77 (Passenger advice bureau at Leeds City in May 1967) John E. Hoggarth; p81 (Sign at Tilbury Riverside November 1985) R. J. S. Owen; p86 (Sign at Dover Prior station on 18 August 1981) John G. Glover; p88 (Tail lamp on southbound freight at Northampton on 23 June 1975) John E. Oxley; p95 (Prophetic sign in Swindon Works on 5 June 1985 prior to closure) Roy Nash; p96 (Station barrier at Fort William during railway dispute in July 1968) T. Mahoney; p100 (Derailed freight train at Dinting on 10 March 1981) Larry Goddard; p101 (A Class 25 breaks through at Stoke on 22 October 1985 B. G. Hughes; p105 (Class 47-hauled train at Garsdale in the snow of 24 April 1981) Eddie Parker; p109 (Dereliction at Notgrove in January 1966) Andrew Muckley; p113 (Ex-GWR brake vans at Highbridge on 28 March 1965) Brian Quemby; p114 (The building of Salford's new station on 1 August 1986) M. F. Haddon; p112 Marconi; p127 (The driver returns to a failed train near Bristol in July 1967) P. J. Fowler; p141 (The fireman of a freight uses the water column at Tebay to put out a wagon that had caught fire on 20 July 1967) G. P. Cooper; 143 C. C. B. ·bert.

385. 1

First published 1996
Reprinted 1996

ISBN 0 7110 2469 3

Published by Ian Allan Publishing

an imprint of Ian Allan Ltd, Terminal House, Station Approach, Shepperton, Surrey TW17 8AS.
Printed by Ian Allan Printing Ltd, Coombelands House, Coombelands Lane, Addlestone, Surrey KT15 1HY.

True stories from the Great Railway Disaster

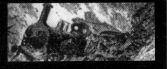

Contents

1. So You Want to Book a Sleeper? 14
2. So You Want to Make a Connection? 16
3. So You Want to Buy the Cheapest Ticket? 18
4. So You Want to See Your Way at Night? 20
5. So You Want to Take Your Bicycle? 22
6. So You Want to Go Abroad by Train? 24
7. So You Want to Get Off the Train? 26
8. So You Want to Travel as a Group? 28
9. So You Want to Use Southport Station? 30
10. So You Want to Catch a Train That Does Not Officially Exist? 32
11. So Railtrack is Being Privatised? 34
12. So You Want to Use Red Star? 36
13. So You Want to Go to Bury St Edmunds? 38
14. So Who Do You Believe? 43
15. So You Want to Use the Toilet? 44
16. So You Want to Use the Toilet? (Part 2) 46
17. So Your Train Needs a Shunt? 48
18. So You Want to Go to Birmingham Slowly? 50
19. So You Want to Buy a Timetable? 52
20. So You Want to Book a Seat on InterCity? 54
21. So You Want an Accurate Timetable for Your Route? 56
22. So You Want to Use a Rival's Train? 58
23. So What's the Fare for the Bicycle? 60
24. So Why Not Just Let the Plane Take the Strain? 62
25. So You Want to Board the Train? 64
26. So You Want to Go to Etchingham? 66
27. So You Want Your Charter Train to Stop at the Stations? 68
28. So You Want to Take the Ghost Train? 70
29. So You Want to Go Further for Less? 72
30. So You Used the Wrong Ticket Machine? 74
31. So You Want The Cheapest Ticket to Birmingham? 76
32. So You Want to Use the Train to Get to Oban for a Cruise? 78
33. So You Want The Full Picture? 80
34. So Competition is a Good Thing? 82
35. So You Want to Use the Eurostar Special? 84

36. So You Want to Get Lost Property Back? 87
37. So You Want Your Station Lit at Night? 88
38. So That's Why the Motorways are Taking the (S)Train? 90
39. So You Want a New Station? 92
40. So You Think We Care if you Missed Your Last Train? 94
41. So You Want to Go the Long Way? 96
42. So You Want to Go the Other Way? 98
43. So That's Why Trains are Going Bumpety Bump in the Night? 100
44. So They Want to Tax Toy Trains? 102
45. So It is the Wrong Type of Snowplough? 104
46. So You Want your Connecting Train to Wait? 106
47. So You Want a Clean Track? 108
48. So You Want to Take a Taxi From the Station? 110
49. So You Want to Charter a Train? 112
50. So You Want to Open a New Station? 114
51. So You Want the Train to Stop at Your Local Station? 116
52. So You Want to Travel as a Group with a Discount? 118
53. So You Want to Get To or From Stockport? 120
54. So You Want the Right Information? 122
55. So You Want New Trains? 124
56. So You Want the Cheapest Fare? 126
57. So You Might as Well Just Take a Taxi? 128
58. So That's Why it's Getting Cramped in the Signalbox? 130
59. So You Want the Right Fare for the Journey? 132
60. So You Want a Local Travelcard for Buses and Trains? 134
61. So There are Too Many People Trying to Use the Trains? 136
62. So That's Why the Trains are Going Bumpety Bump (Part 2) 138
63. So You Want to Use the Fire Extinguisher? 140
64. So You Need to Know Who the Guard Works For? 142

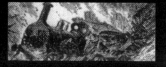

Introduction

The scene: The Department of Transport, Marsham Street in Whitehall.

The date: 1995

The players: A number of senior rail managers, civil servants and a key transport minister.

The plan: To produce a document outlining the advantages of rail privatisation.

'Well,' asks the minister, 'let's bounce a few ideas around. Why are we privatising the railways?'

Silence.

'Well, surely that's not too difficult. It's to provide improved services for passengers.'

'Ah, minister,' replies one of the civil servants, 'at the moment things have deteriorated and they had been improving rapidly under the old system.'

'Well, then, let's say it's to improve competition. That, after all, is the main purpose, isn't it?'

'Ah, minister,' replies an even braver flunkey, 'we've actually stopped competition being introduced because otherwise no one would buy the franchises as rival operators could come and pinch the best routes and times.'

'Well, then, it's to save money and make it more efficient.'

'Ah, minister,' replies the bravest of them all, 'British Rail has shed 25,000 jobs over three years with barely a fuss from the unions and no strikes. And privatisation has cost several hundred million so far because of the reorganisation and fees for consultants and lawyers. I don't think that would go down too well.'

'Well, then, let's just say we're privatising the railways, shall we?'

This tale was recounted by a former senior railway manager, angered like so many at what had been done to the railway in the years between 1992 and 1996 when it was being prepared for privatisation. The story may have been embellished over time, which is why the names of the main actors have been removed, but in essence it is true. It demonstrates what all observers of the rail industry already know — that the privatisation of the railways was carried out for ideological rather than practical reasons.

It was the privatisation that even Mrs Thatcher shied away from. For good reason. The railways are not only deeply loved, but they are also deeply subsidised. Making them private will not take away the need for massive amounts of public money and therefore rail privatisation is unlike any other.

Mrs Thatcher's government had kicked around one or two models for rail privatisation, but they had been rejected. The fiasco over the poll tax was enough to put ministers off further radical reforms. But in the run-up to the 1992 general election, Malcolm Rifkind, a wettish Tory, wanted to show that he was 'one of us' and drew up a draft scheme for privatisation. John Major had wanted the restoration of the big consolidated companies which had operated between 1923 and 1948 and whose evocative names — such as London Midland, Scottish and Great Western Railway — had lived on within the nationalised railway during his boyhood. Even if he wasn't a trainspotter, and there is nothing to suggest he was, he must have seen the mighty engines of that era and with his penchant for nostalgia, it was hardly surprising that he fancied the idea of restoring these great companies. (Actually they never made any money and led a troubled existence from start to finish, but that's another story.)

But he was talked out of it by something much more radical developed by Rifkind and his adviser Sir Christopher Foster. The cornerstone of the idea was the franchising out of rail services to a host of small companies. At the time numbers as high as 40 were mooted, but later in the process it turned out to be 25.

The White Paper 'New Opportunities for the Railways, the privatisation of British Rail' makes hairy reading. There was, for example, no commitment to guarantee through ticketing: 'It will be for train service operators to make arrangements to accept each other's tickets,' it says. Travelcards and railcards were to be a matter of 'commercial interest'. In fact, as with many such measures, the hard radical edge of such notions was blunted by the realities of politics. People want through ticketing, Railcards and other network benefits, and these have now largely been guaranteed by the Government. Yet, as this book shows, a number of anomalies have been created and many uncertainties remain.

After the Conservative victory at the April 1992 election, in which rail privatisation was a manifesto commitment, ministers moved swiftly. As with everything to do with rail privatisation, they moved with breakneck speed, knowing that it had to be done quickly in order to begin to show the benefits of privatisation by the time of the next general election, which had to be held in the spring of 1997 at the latest.

The ignorance of the railway industry and of the complexity facing the Government is illustrated by the promise of Roger Freeman, the transport minister, to get trains in the private sector by the spring of 1994. Ministers pooh-poohed the managers in the rail industry who tried to slow the rate of change, knowing that the railways had just gone through the largely-successful organising for quality reorganisation which had led to the creation of three rail businesses: InterCity, Regional Railways and Network SouthEast. Now having just relaxed into the new structure, all managers could foresee was yet more reorganisation and chaos. They even sent a delegation to Marsham Street, the HQ of the Department of Transport, begging for more time and a say in the reorganisation.

Of course they got more time, not because of any generosity on the Government's part, but because the task was simply too enormous. The first privatised trains did not run until 4 February

1996, nearly two years later than Mr Freeman's schedule — and then the first service was actually a bus replacing a train because of engineering works — and politically embarrassing since that left little time for the famed 'benefits of privatisation' to show through. No matter how many times Sir George Young, the transport secretary, said 'This is a great day for rail passengers,' no one believed him. The few promises of new trains and improvements to stations made by the privatised train operating companies were for the future, beyond the last possible date for a general election.

That is not to say that everything to do with privatisation is bad. Certainly, it seems a good idea to get some private sector skills involved in marketing trains. BR's weakness has always been selling, though its marketing has improved enormously over the years with its more sophisticated ticket pricing, such as Savers and Apex returns. Moreover, selling off the railfreight industry in an effort to make it more competitive with road haulage has been widely welcomed. There is, too, an advantage in introducing private sector disciplines into the railways' industrial relations. Despite BR's much improved productivity over the past decade, making BR one of the most efficient railways in the world, there is still room for further improvements. But so there is in privatised industries such as BT and the water authorities, and the Post Office has shown that nationalised companies can become enormously profitable and efficient while staying in the public sector.

Sir Bob Reid, the chairman of BR who had to preside over the

The Tories' 'scorched earth' policy revealed.

dismemberment of the structures which he had created and which appeared to be delivering massive improvements in productivity and performance, resisted strenuously the privatisation model which ministers had designed. He suggested a number of alternatives, notably contracting out the maintenance and infrastructure work which he knew would lead to great savings. But he was ignored.

Instead, the Government ploughed on with what has become the most controversial of all the privatisations initiated by the Tories since 1979. It is immensely complex, so much so that it is like the story told about the Schleswig-Holstein question to which only three people knew the answer; one was mad, one was dead and the third had forgotten. (Reader: skip the next few paragraphs if you don't want the technical details.)

Briefly, the structure goes something like this: the old BR has been broken up into 25 train operating companies, Railtrack, 13 maintenance and track renewal companies, three rolling stock companies, and a host of smaller organisations ranging from design firms to Sparesco, which is entirely concerned with providing spare parts.

The train operating companies which run the rail services are being franchised out to the private sector. All require subsidy and therefore the private operator offering to run the service for the least subsidy gets the contract which is allocated by the franchising director, Roger Salmon. Mr Salmon has set minimum passenger service requirements (PSRs) for each line. These specify which trains the operator is obliged to run. Most loss-making services have been specified, although many early and late trains have not been included and InterCity services to some towns such as Carmarthen and Fishguard have not been included in the requirements. Many so-called commercially viable trains have not been included, because Mr Salmon says that these would be run anyway without the need for his subsidy. The precise arrangements over the PSRs led to a court case in December 1995 which was a partial victory for the anti-privatisation campaigners who forced Sir George Young to issue new guidance about the way PSRs were drawn up, but it failed to stop the first franchises from passing into the private sector.

Railtrack has taken over all the parts of the rail network which do not move. It owns all the 2,500 stations, the track, the signalling systems and all the associated railway property. Originally, the idea was to keep it in the private sector until all the franchises had been let, but ministers then cottoned on to the fact that its sale would help pay for tax cuts. The chairman, Bob Horton, was also keen to privatise it as quickly as possible and therefore it was due to be sold just as this book is being published. Railtrack contracts services from the 13 maintenance and track renewal companies which should all have been privatised by the time this book is published.

The rolling stock companies (Roscos) were sold for £1.8 billion in December 1995 and own all the passenger trains and locomotives. They make their money by leasing the trains to the train operating companies and are, so far, the only suppliers of trains and coaches to them, although eventually it is envisaged that manufacturers may supply equipment direct to the operators.

The process is overseen by two organisations: the Office of Passenger Rail Franchising, headed by Mr Salmon; and the Office of the Rail Regulator, headed by John Swift QC. Mr Salmon draws up the minimum standards, puts the lines out to tender, chooses the franchisee and ensures the smooth transfer. Mr Swift is required to protect the interests of passengers and also ensure that there are no anti-competitive practices on the railways.

There are many objections to this model which are worth summing up quickly. First, it created a very high cost network. Railtrack has to make a good return on its assets and so do the rolling stock companies. They have both been fattened up with some £700 million extra subsidy each year — from a total of £1.1 billion to £1.8 billion — to ensure that they can be sold off to the private sector. This not only discourages operators from providing extra trains, but means that high rates of subsidy will have to be paid for evermore by future governments. The fact that it would be cost-effective for a future Labour government to buy back Railtrack is one of the most important arguments in favour of it. It would also need to regulate the Roscos which have been left out of the regulatory control of Mr Swift and therefore have total freedom to spend all their excess profits, which means that like the privatised water companies, they could embark on any kind of wasteful diversification. Nor does

the new financial structure take into account the social benefits of the railway. Everything has to be costed in terms of whether an investment can make an adequate return in purely financial terms. There is no one to look at the overall picture and to place rail transport within the context of offering an alternative to our overcrowded and congested roads.

Secondly, the sheer complexity of the new structure, as outlined above, is extremely wasteful. Just as the NHS reforms have created an unnecessary bureaucracy, so has rail privatisation. There has literally been an army of lawyers and consultants brought in to the railway to draw up the privatisation scheme, and many will be employed for years to try to sort out the mess.

The creation of 25 train operating companies was, simply, ridiculous. It was only done in order to make them small enough to sell and to instil a notion of competition, but mergers and acquisitions are bound to follow, and if the process is allowed to run its course, most commentators suggest there will be only half a dozen companies by the turn of the decade. The waste is impossible to estimate, but its extent is nicely illustrated by the separation in 1994 of the three railfreight companies which were supposed to compete with each other. Yet, in early 1996, they were sold together to Wisconsin Central, which meant that all the money spent on separate management teams and all the paraphernalia such as logos and 'corporate identities' were wasted. The same thing will happen with passenger services.

Thirdly, the separation of Railtrack

from the train operators is a very radical idea which most rail managers still, two years on, oppose. While legally, according to the European Union, some technical separation had to be made, actually selling off Railtrack, on which all train operators fundamentally depend, is an untested idea which logic dictates will lead to a deterioration in services. Already, in the first year of separation, reliability and punctuality declined markedly.

Fourthly, unlike every other privatisation, the railways will remain dependent on government subsidy. The notion of large amounts of taxpayers' money going into the pockets of private shareholders is a nonsense.

Finally, there is the point made at the beginning of this introduction. What is the privatisation for? One of the constant refrains was to introduce competition on to the railways. But the railways are merely a means of transport and face enormous competition from the car and, for some journeys, air. There is no need for on-rail competition and as the Government quickly discovered, it is virtually impossible to stimulate it in any meaningful way. One of John Swift's first actions was to ban competition against franchisees from so-called 'open access' operators because he realised that if rival companies were allowed to cherry-pick the best trains, no one would take on a franchise. Therefore, the whole structure was created to stimulate something which has now been banned. It makes a nonsense of the very structure of privatisation and even most supporters of privatisation will admit, in private, that they have not found a way

round that contradiction. It is the most fundamental flaw in the whole process. Many of the changes have been introduced in the dogmatic search for greater competition. And yet, there is to be very little on-rail competition. Rather than going back to the drawing board and coming up with a more sustainable form of privatisation, ministers kept on building their edifice, regardless of the fact that the bottom layer of bricks had been removed.

It is not surprising, therefore, that opposition to privatisation has come from all kinds of unexpected quarters. The late Tory MP, Robert Adley, a great friend of the railways, called it a 'poll tax on wheels' while the normally mild-speaking Major General Lennox-Napier in his departing speech as head of CRUCC, the rail watchdog, called privatisation a 'pantomime' without a happy ending. The opinion polls have shown that around 80% of the population oppose privatisation and that it has influenced many people's voting intentions. To get so many people to rally around in support of British Rail is, arguably, the greatest achievement of rail privatisation so far. Government spokespeople are so desperate for any reports praising — or even merely not criticising — rail privatisation that when a journalist writes or broadcasts something nice about it, the various press officers at the Department of Transport argue about who should claim credit for the positive coverage.

Of course, with the Labour party vociferously opposed to privatisation and the bulk of the British public extremely sceptical about it, the Government has been given a very rough ride. To some extent this has been unfair because, as I wrote in 1992, 'every leaf on the line will be blamed on privatisation'. Mostly, however, the Government got its just desserts. The privatisation scheme was driven by dogma and the structure of the scheme is too complex and bureaucratic. It does nothing to stimulate investment and ensures that rail is priced very heavily compared with travel by rail. Roads are not, for example, expected to provide an onerous return on their costs, as railways now are. There were some good ideas such as ensuring there is a proper performance regime to monitor punctuality and reliability. It is also laudable to monitor costs and to make them 'transparent', although at times it costs more to find out the cost of something than it actually costs!

This is a punters' book — with three or four exceptions, all these items have been contributed by readers of the Independent on Sunday. The exceptions are issues which came to light widely in the press. Many of the 'Mad' column items themselves have been taken up by radio and TV programmes and by other newspapers. The Daily Mirror in fact printed a whole page of them.

For those familiar with the 'Mad' column, you will see lots of additions and all the famous rail privatisation fiascos are included — the Fort William sleeper, the 300 ticket selling stations plan, the London, Tilbury and Southend Travelcard fiddle which resulted in the franchise being delayed, the 56% rise because of overcrowding and so on. And all this is happening before privatisation has even started in earnest.

Some of the items may not be directly attributed to privatisation, but virtually all are a result of the increased commercialisation of the railways. Decisions are being taken which in narrow financial terms may be sensible but, when viewed in a larger context, are patently ridiculous. Some items arose because of the stroppiness of particular officials, others because of the structures created for privatisation. There are many recurring themes such as petty rivalries and the need for all the new players in the railway to maximise their revenue. And all these tales have one point in common — the journey was made less pleasant or more difficult as a result of the changes made since the railways were prepared for privatisation.

The 'Mad' column has proved a useful threat. Not only have there been several victories as a result of items raised in it, its very existence has rattled the cages of all the senior players in the rail privatisation saga. Both ministers and the franchising director, Roger Salmon, have asked to respond to the column because they fear it has undermined privatisation. Behind the scenes, too, the issues raised by the column have been addressed in meetings at the Department of Transport. And the very threat of sending material to the 'Mad' column has resulted in railway officials being more helpful. Passengers have apparently started threatening staff with appearances in the 'Mad' column, only to find that their problems are quickly resolved. So, make sure you carry this book with you everywhere you go on the network and make sure you keep sending items to Christian Wolmar, 'Mad', the Independent on Sunday, 1 Canada Square, London E14 5DL.

February 1996

'Don't talk to me about the wrong sort of snow.'

Ian Jack wanted to travel on the sleeper train from Euston to Glasgow and tried to make a late booking. At around 8.30pm on 13 January 1995, he telephoned Euston to find out if there was a free berth on that night's train. There were still two hours before the sleeper was due to leave, but he found that the information was 'not available'.

He was told that the reason was 'restructuring'. The sleepers have, for many years, been the responsibility of the West Coast main line division of British Rail, but under reorganisation they were due to be handed over to ScotRail in May 1995. The trains will, in fact, continue to be run by InterCity West Coast but the administration of the sleeper service will be the responsibility of ScotRail. Hence, a stall to help passengers understand this new complexity was set up on the Euston concourse. Once the computer list has been handed over on the day of travel, sleeper reservations are taken only at this concourse stall. It does not, of course, have a telephone.

Update: The sleeper services were indeed handed over to ScotRail in May 1995. But thanks to a successful campaign by the friends of the West Highland Line, the proposal to axe the service to Fort William had to be scrapped. The campaigners fought a legal battle in the courts over technical aspects of the closure and after they won the case, the franchising director and the Government caved in, ensuring that the service would remain open.

Response: In February 1996, ScotRail wrote in great detail in response to a request for an explanation. Eddie Toal, of ScotRail, said: 'We have absolutely no idea why Mr Jack was unable to find out if there were berths available on the Glasgow sleeper when he phoned at 8.30pm in January 1995. We have no record of ever having received a complaint, so I can't check to see what telephone number he rang. To put all this down to something called 'restructuring' simply sounds like "b******s" to me because ScotRail didn't even take over the sleepers until May 1995.

'As far as the Glasgow train is concerned, the Euston telesales can take phone credit card bookings until shortly before 10pm. After that the list closes and is handed over to the sleeping car attendant who proceeds to the train to make preliminary checks on bed make-up, food stocks, etc, before being on hand to welcome passengers. He is, therefore, the only person who can make reservation transactions after the list has closed. This is to avoid the risk of double booking on busy trains by people by-passing the booking office.'

Mr Toal continues: 'I have to confess that despite all the problems we've had since taking over the sleepers (and there have been plenty, both political and logistical) we haven't received any complaints about inability to make late bookings.'

But then just in case: 'That said, as a result of your item, we are going to investigate the possibility of issuing a "first edition" list to the sleeping car attendant and taking later reservations at the terminal booking office until, say, 15min before departure whereupon the "final edition" list would be handed over to the attendant to permit last minute bookings.'

Mr Toal added that ScotRail was planning to introduce a hotline which will enable sleeper reservations to be sold via one UK telephone number for the price of a local call.

Comment: A 'Mad' victory perhaps, given that Scotrail is considering new arrangements.

'Good morning, Madam. I trust that you had a good journey and that you weren't inconvenienced by the late arrival of the journalist who's sleeping under your bed.'

2. So You Want to Make a Connection?

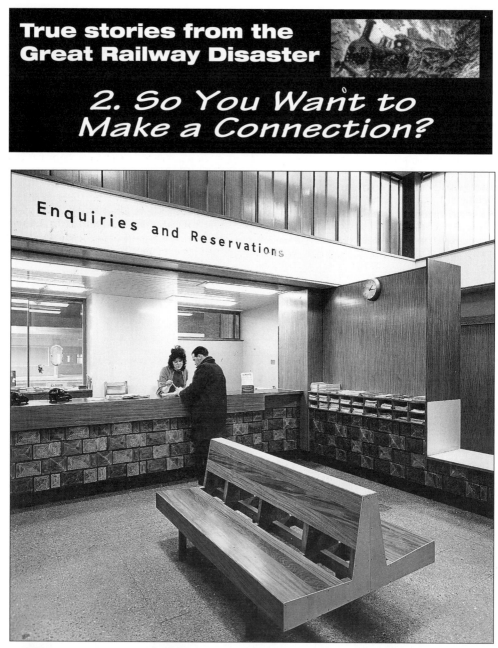

Enquiries and Reservations

'Well, on Thursdays when there's an 'R' in the month the fare is £10.95; but normally the Thursday fare would be £12.60. However, in December the Thursday fare is only £9.90 because of the special pre-Christmas sale.'

There are, in the new British railways, the official and the unofficial, especially when it comes to connecting trains. Paul Gosling was travelling from Leicester to Manchester, changing at Sheffield and was delayed because his connection was an 'unofficial' one. His train was due in at 09.11 at Sheffield and the Manchester train was due to leave at 09.14. Eight other passengers joined Mr Gosling in the race from platform three to platform eight only to see the Manchester train pulling out. Mr Gosling complained to the station manager who looked unsurprised. The official explained that he could not have delayed the departure because the train Mr Gosling had arrived on was run by InterCity while the departing one was operated by Regional Railways North West. One company's train could not be delayed leaving to await a train run by another company.

Mr Gosling was told he would have to wait for the 'official' connecting train which was scheduled to leave almost half an hour later. Mr Gosling suggested this was crazy and the station manager 'tried to look, successfully, as if he agreed with me'. Mr Gosling asked if it would help if he wrote to complain, but was told 'it would be of no use whatsoever'.

It was not Mr Gosling's only experience with the 'new railway', as ministers call it. He goes on: 'We all know that the train system has gone loopy, but it continues to amaze me. I obtained a £5 refund the other day because the train guide for the East Midlands contained details of trains that did not exist, and omitted details of trains that do, having created a false category of "Monday only" trains.' He explained the problem to the guard who said that he knew about the problem, but weeks later the guide containing the errors was still in print.

Then Mr Gosling was phoned up by an opinion pollster working for BR who asked him questions like whether it was important to have a toilet on the train and at stations, and whether there should be disabled access. He writes: 'When I explained that what I really wanted to tell them was that they needed extra phone lines for train service information as I could never get through, and that they should allow bikes on to trains again, I was told there were no boxes on the pollsters form for these points and they could not be included in the survey.'

Mr Gosling was then rung by another researcher who phoned to ask if he had been satisfied with the manner of the first pollster: 'When I tried to tell them about my complaints not being responded to, I was told that it was outside the scope of this research. It is like living in the middle of a Franz Kafka novel.'

Response: We wrote to Regional Railways North West and to InterCity Midland but no reply has been received.

Comment: This is a source of great irritation among contributors to the 'Mad' column who have sent in many other examples — see, for example, No 46.

3. So You Want to Buy the Cheapest Ticket?

Through ticketing is already a thing of the past, if the experience of Rose Harvie is anything to go by. She wanted to buy a London to Glasgow return ticket at her local station, Dumbarton Central. During the recent furore over through-ticketing, it was implied that currently any type of ticket could be bought at all stations. But when Mrs Harvie told the ticket clerk at Dumbarton that she wanted to purchase a Super Apex return from Glasgow to London, costing £29 if booked two weeks in advance, she was told that it was not possible. Instead, the booking clerk offered an Apex return for £44 if booked one week in advance.

Mrs Harvie pointed out that the leaflet on travel between Scotland and London said the ticket can be purchased 'at most staffed stations' but she was told that to do so she would have to travel to Glasgow at a cost of £2.70 to buy the cheaper ticket. She also discovered that she could buy the Super Apex at a local travel agent, but would have to pay a £2 booking fee.

Her letter of complaint to Scotrail was passed on to InterCity West Coast in Birmingham who failed to respond. When she rang to complain, Mrs Harvie was first put through to the catering department, and then the recruitment section. When she finally got through to 'customer relations' she was told that her letter had 'got lost' but after some argument, they found it. She eventually received a response from a customer relations officer, Steve Perry, who wrote: 'Super Apex tickets are not available from Dumbarton station (because) the station is controlled by the Strathclyde Passenger Transport Executive. There is not enough demand for this ticket to warrant the costs involved. I am unable to comment further on this matter and I am sorry that I cannot go into any more detail on this subject.' Despite this reluctance to discuss the matter, he still looked forward to 'welcoming you on board again in the near future'.

Update: This was yet another of the great victories for the 'Mad' railways column. Mrs Harvie later told us that following our item on her problem in getting the right ticket, Mr Perry wrote to her saying this was a result of 'a misunderstanding that should not have arisen'. Enclosing a £10 voucher for travel, he said that she would now be able to buy the required ticket at Dumbarton. This was in marked contrast to his previous letter which had said 'I am unable to comment further on this matter'.

A similar dispute arose in early 1996 when Scotrail withdrew through tickets sales from smaller stations where previously it had been possible to buy tickets for journeys on InterCity. The reason was that Scotrail is, under new regulations, forced to specify exactly when its ticket offices are open. Apparently, some of its staff are not trained to sell the full range of tickets and therefore it could not guarantee that InterCity tickets would be available at all times. Therefore, it decided to withdraw all facilities for such sales, but it was rebuked by the Rail Regulator after the matter was brought to his attention by Save our Railways campaigners and Scotrail was forced to reinstate the full service.

Comment: The plan — which stimulated the furore referred to above — by the rail regulator, John Swift, to restrict to 300 the number of stations where tickets for the whole network could be bought was quietly shelved after a public outcry. Nevertheless, ticket inter-availability or non-availability remains one of the most fraught issues of the rail privatisation process.

'Look. Can you tell me whether it is cheaper to buy a Super Apex, an ordinary Apex, a Saver return, a Super Saver return, a day return or an ordinary single? After all I only want to get to the next station!'

Ruth Morgan had complained several times about half a dozen broken light bulbs on the approach to her local station, Barnes, in southwest London. She had first noticed that the street lights on a narrow road next to Barnes Common were not working in November 1994. She says 'I would not consider myself paranoid about being attacked' but just had 'a heightened awareness of the possibility in such an area'. Therefore, she felt she ought to contact British Rail to inform them that half the street lights were not working. She was told by the 'customer service' department of the local train operating company, South West Trains, that she would have to put the complaint in writing and it would be dealt with promptly.

Not so. Her first letter was not answered for a month and when she remonstrated with South West Trains, she was told that the delay was caused by management not being sure about who owned the lights. Although the lights were of the same type as those on all the local stations, which suggested they were BR property, she was told in response to a second letter that they might be owned by South West Trains, Railtrack, or the local council. One division of the newly fragmented railway could not overstep its limits and replace the lights if they were not its responsibility. When Ms Morgan asked whether this was not a bit bureaucratic for the sake of a few light bulbs, she was told 'it is an effect of privatisation'.

She was told a letter would be sent informing her of any action taken as soon as possible. In mid-January, she was sent a letter informing her that the manager of Barnes station would be looking into the matter. As the spring of 1995 approached, the alley was still in darkness. Ms Morgan commented: 'I should have bought and replaced the light bulbs myself for piece of mind rather than waiting for dithering management to decide whose responsibility they were. Obviously passenger security or a basic service are not priorities for BR or, ultimately, the Government.'

Update: Ms Morgan struggled all winter to try to get the lights fixed on the alleyway but failed. She said that by the time she stopped using the line regularly in mid-summer 1995, the bulbs had still not replaced. Ms Morgan then left for Canada, presumably to avoid having to travel on British trains, but in January 1996 her father kindly went to Barnes station on behalf of the 'Mad' column to check whether the lights were working and found the alley in deep gloom since only four of the eight lamps were functioning.

Response: Railtrack's press officer Kate Smyth provided the following explanation: 'The responsibility for light bulbs belongs to either South West Trains or the local authority depending on which part of the road we're talking about. If it is a part of road owned by Railtrack then though Railtrack would be responsible for major work on the lighting, replacing bulbs is the duty of the leasee (sic) as it is when you rent a flat.'

The station lighting office at Barnes prepares its allocation of individual lights for the arrival of the season ticket holders. A spokesperson commented: 'We only have enough lights for season ticket holders and those who book in advance; others, I am afraid, will have to make their own lighting arrangements.'

5: So You Want to Take Your Bicycle?

Cyclists and cycling groups have long been campaigning for better access to trains for bicycles. However, with the introduction of many new trains that do not have guard's vans or have space for just one bike, the situation has been getting worse as David Keep of Crewkerne in Somerset recently found out. In January 1995, he travelled by train from his local station to visit a friend near Newmarket. He wanted to take his cycle as the house he was visiting is eight miles from Newmarket station. As South West Trains were unable to sell him a through ticket to Newmarket, he bought a return to Cambridge and the bicycle was taken at a cost of £3 each way.

When he got to Cambridge, he bought a ticket to Newmarket but was told that he would have to ask the 'driver' about the bicycle as there was a limit of one per train. However, when he went to take the train, the guard refused him entry as Anglia Railways had recently introduced a new regulation banning all cycles at peak times because, apparently, 'of the possible danger to other passengers'. It left him with the choice of waiting two and a half hours or cycling 22 miles. He was forced to resort to a taxi big enough to fit his bike in the boot.

When he complained, he was told that Anglia had tried to be more lenient with its policy of carrying cycles but 'the difficulty is that on these services we have one carriage and two-carriage trains. Both these trains are used on all services at both peak and off-peak times. Therefore the policy had to be geared to the train with the least amount of storage space. This being the one-carriage train.'

In fact there was plenty of room for Mr Keep on the train as it was a two-carriage train. He wrote: 'I have the current leaflet about bicycles on trains. It does not mention Anglia Railways' new regulation. The staff at Cambridge did not generally appear to be aware either.'

He raises a wider issue about the nature of the train network and the type of service it provides. He wrote: 'Although I have a car, travel by bicycle and train is my preferred mode on grounds of convenience, comfort, cost and environmental consideration.' Will users of the rail system like Mr Keep be accommodated in future?

Update/response: Anglia Railways replied at great length to the coverage of Mr Keep's complaint. Jonathan Denby, the public relations manager, blamed financial restrictions when the rolling stock was first ordered and seemed to be arguing that attracting cyclists to the railway cost too much money. He said: 'When Regional Railways nationally, as it then was, was commissioning new rolling stock in 1986/7, it was working with extremely restricted budgets and was looking for cost-effective trains both in terms of operational reliability and efficient space utilisation (Author's note: why do bureaucrats always say "utilise" rather than the much better word "use"?). As a result the varied types of new generation rolling stock introduced from 1987 onwards have had very little space for bicycles from the day they were built. Irrespective of the many diverse views on the optimum space for bicycles on trains, the fact remains that they were built to the current design and have operated with the same layout from their first day in full service to the present day. Restrictions on bicycle carriage have therefore been necessary particularly at peak times.'

Mr Denby then argues that bikes pose a hazard to other passengers: 'It would be completely unacceptable for any of our passengers to be injured by a falling or moving bicycle which... may be a risk on a peak time train where there are more travellers and less space to move around in.' He goes on to say that these restrictions have been in place for four years, but fails to address Mr Keep's point which is that different train companies are unaware of each other's various rules on bikes and even Anglia staff themselves seemed to be confused about the rules. In any case, cycling groups respond that few trains are so full that bikes present any risk — which in any case is very low, as demonstrated on, say, suburban services in Amsterdam where people and bikes mix freely. The groups suggest that discretion could be used especially as Anglia's response implies that there is space on the train when two carriages are being used.

Mr Denby does end on a positive note, saying: 'We now have a team set up to find an effective, safe, sustainable and robust way of addressing the issue of space for bicycles on our local services. As this may ultimately involve modifications to the trains, there is no instant solution, but we are being proactive in trying to deal with this particular issue.'

However, by January 1996, when we wrote to Mr Denby asking for any new information, he was sounding a lot more upbeat about bikes and seemed to have changed his tune. He said: 'We are currently taking a number of steps to improve the provision of space for bicycles on trains and at stations. We are leading an initiative with the support of Suffolk, Norfolk and Cambridgeshire County Councils to modify our entire fleet of local trains to carry more bicycles. A submission led by Suffolk County Council on behalf of Anglia (and Norfolk and Cambridgeshire) has been successful in securing £75,000 towards the cost of the scheme. The plan is to have a prototype ready in May/June 1996, followed by modification of the entire local fleet of trains over the subsequent six months. Two-carriage trains will be able to carry six bicycles, while single-carriage ones could carry four bicycles. Once the local trains have been modified, the aim is to review pricing for bicycles on local journeys and actively promote the improved facilities for cyclists using the train. If our initiative is successful, it will be a template for other local train services across the network.

'In addition, provision for bicycles is already being upgraded at stations with special secure bicycle lockers at Ipswich and Norwich.'

Another victory for 'Mad'.

CYCLIST ACCESS

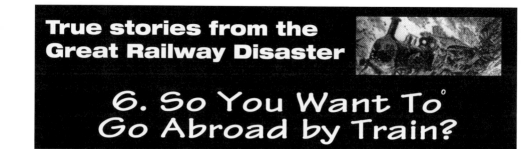

True stories from the Great Railway Disaster

6. So You Want To Go Abroad by Train?

Since the Eurostar Channel Tunnel trains started running in the autumn of 1994, people can travel by train from London to Paris and Brussels and, by changing, to the rest of Europe. Alan Harrison of Walsall in the West Midlands went to his local station to see if he could book a journey to Italy. No chance, he was told, he would have to go to Birmingham New Street.

Mr Harrison phoned New Street. However, although it is the biggest station on the rail network outside the capital, he was told that international

enquiries could not be dealt with by phone and that only Victoria in London offered this service. Mr Harrison comments: 'The station is the British equivalent of Lyon Perrache or Milano Centrale, yet it is not equipped to deal with a simple telephone enquiry about international trains.' He adds that it should have had a direct through service by early 1995 had the tunnel opened on time and the trains been ready.

Mr Harrison, who regularly takes international train journeys, feels that despite the Channel Tunnel, railway travel to the Continent has got more difficult, rather than easier: 'As recently as 1981, I was able to get a through ticket from Walsall to Paris while a friend remembers his father being able to ask for two and two halves return from Walsall to Naples!' He recalls that BR used to publish a continental timetable: 'I have not seen it for several years. Do they want us to go by train?'

Mr Harrison at least found that staff at New Street dealt with his enquiry 'very efficiently', and confirmed that their phone 'had been taken out in an economy drive'.

Response: A BR spokesman confirmed that it had stopped publishing a continental timetable in 1988 and there were no plans to start issuing one again despite the opening of the Channel Tunnel.

Left: 'And so you want to go to Paris? ... Yes, if I were you I'd get a train from Calais. I know the Channel Tunnel has opened but ... '

Above: Reflecting the lack of maintenance facilities, a Class 37 is jump-started in the open air.

7. So You Want to Get Off the Train?

Getting off trains is not always easy, as two passengers discovered. David Bayton, seeking to travel from Aberystwyth to Edinburgh wanted to drop off to see a friend at Lancaster on the way. At Aberystwyth station, he was told that it would be possible to break the journey on the way back, but not on the way there. The clerk was unable to tell Mr Bayton why. When he sent a letter to Midland BR customer services, 'they wrote a rather sharpish letter back saying it was a business decision'. Mr Bayton went by car. 'Some business decision,' he comments.

Dr John Patterson's experience was rather different. He was helping his pregnant wife on to a train at Newark only to find that the door would not open when he tried to get off and found himself having to go to Retford. He sought the guard and while looking for him met a passenger, travelling with two young children, who had tried to leave the train at Newark. Her ten-year-old son had got off the train, but she and her younger son were not quick enough. The door closed between her and her eldest boy. (Fortunately, the woman's parents were waiting for her and were able to look after the boy who had got off.)

The guard of the train was standing next to her but refused to help her. He also told Dr Patterson that there were 'lots of signs' at Newark telling the public that they should not board a train if they do not intend to travel on it. But when Dr Patterson returned to Newark after his unintended journey, he found no such signs. He was told by the local station official that the signs had been taken down because 'people ignored them'. In his letter of complaint to InterCity East Coast, Dr Patterson comments: 'It seems to me that the frustration and fear that was imposed on me and my fellow sufferer was a result of attempts to achieve targets in terms of "timing" and "economy". I urge you to resist such attempts — your "customers" are people.'

Response/comment: Neither of these cases is strictly related to privatisation, though Dr Patterson's experience was clearly as a result of increasing commercial pressures on the railway which are a prelude to privatisation.

As for Mr Bayton, BR says this is a commercial decision. 'If people want to make these complicated journeys, then it is probably essential for them, and therefore they will be happy to pay the higher fares.' An odd bit of logic.

'Personally, I've always found it easier to get out from a train when Railtrack provide a platform.'

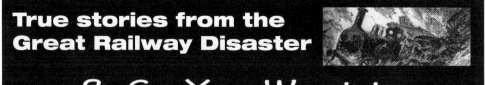
8. So You Want to Travel as a Group?

Frank Fearn, a schoolteacher in Frome, Somerset, has taken a group of two dozen 12- and 13-year-olds and four teachers to the Peak District for a four-day trip each May since 1990. A rail enthusiast, he has always taken the group on the 07.09 from Frome to Bristol where they changed for Derby. This year, for insurance reasons, he had to book the journey through the Youth Hostels Association which advised him to hire a coach because of the hassle involved in dealing with the railways.

Mr Fearn wanted to fight the railways' corner and insisted he wanted to go by train, but found out why the YHA was reluctant to deal with the railways.

Previously the service had been run by BR's Regional Railways division, but it has now become the responsibility of South Wales and West Railways who told the YHA they did not want Mr Fearn's business because the 07.09 train, the only one with the right connection, was 'too busy'.

He was told that his group would have to catch a very early train (the 06.40am) and change at Westbury. Mr Fearn, unwilling to subject his party to a third change, asked if they could stand up in the train or even 'huddle together in a corner, but no, if we all turned up one at a time and pretended we were not a party, we would be all right. They did agree, however, that if the group all turned up as individuals and pretended not to be together, it would be alright, "but no parties were to be had on the 07.09".'

Response: Chris Gibb, manager of Western Cross County South Wales and West Railway Ltd, said that he declined to allow the group to use the 07.09 because there was insufficient capacity as it is a morning commuter train. He adds: 'Group travel attracts a 25% discount but there are, and always have been, some limits on which trains can be used. Most groups we handle travel on the train of their choice. This is not connected with privatisation in any way.'

Comment: Clearly the change in policy *is* connected with privatisation since Mr Fearn had happily used that train for several years previously and it was the separation of BR into 25 train operating companies which resulted in the change in policy.

Left: In an effort to get round the ban on their use of the 7.09 service, pupils build their own train.

Above: In an endeavour to attract a more youthful customer, Railtrack learns from the theme park business and introduces its own version of a roller-coaster.

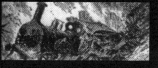
9. So You Want to Use Southport Station?

Privatisation has led to a number of bewildering changes for users of Southport station according to Noel Harvey of Ormskirk. The station serves two destinations: Liverpool with trains provided by Merseyrail Electrics, and Manchester with trains from Regional Railways. It is owned by Railtrack but

leased to Merseyrail which is responsible for it.

To passengers, the first indication of the change in December 1994 was the separation of the platforms and entrances. Platforms 1 to 4 are assigned to Merseyrail, while 5 and 6 are for RR trains. A barrier has been erected to separate the two groups of platforms and the Regional Railways passengers have now been blocked from using the main station concourse and have to enter via a back way. Platform 4, however, cannot be used by Merseyrail trains since it is not electrified and all the Merseyrail trains are electric.

Angus Keith, a regular user of Southport station, says that the separation of the two parts of the station means that making train connections can be very hairy: 'The Regional Railways service is pretty infrequent and if I am connecting with a train from the Merseyrail service, I tend to get an earlier train, because you have to go out of the barriers, leave the concourse, and re-enter the station through a side entrance to reach platforms 5 and 6. It only takes a couple of minutes, but that can make all the difference to getting your train.'

Some RR services are provided using locomotive-hauled carriages. When these trains are prepared for the return journey, the locomotives now have to go through a much more complicated shunting procedure because they are no longer able to use Platform 3 for this manoeuvre as that platform is now leased by Merseyrail.

Delays and cancellations are being increased because of the split between the two organisations. Mr Harvey says: 'Any RR train needing the attention of a fitter or other specialist will not be handled by ME staff who, prior to 1 January 1994, were perfectly capable of doing so; now, however, such attention, no matter how small, must await the arrival of personnel from the RR base at Wigan. Such people will arrive (hopefully) on the next service, ie some 40–60min later, thus delaying (and probably causing the cancellation) of the departure of the faulty train which should have been the next service for Manchester.'

While there are Merseyrail staff at Southport, RR has decided to 'destaff' its part of the station, and RR passengers cannot ask for help from the Merseyrail staff for say, help with getting up the stairs if they are disabled. The Merseyrail staff do, at least, provide train information to RR passengers.

Mr Harvey comments: 'Drivers and other rail staff must, by now, be totally convinced that they are working for "fantasy railways".'

Update: There have been other similar examples sent to the 'Mad' railway column, but this was by far the best one.

Response: We wrote to both Regional Railways North West and to Merseyrail Electrics, but no reply has been received.

Southport. Abandon hope, all ye who enter here.

10. So You Want to Catch a Train That Does Not Officially Exist?

As the rail network is split into 25 train operating companies, 'rival' operators are increasingly leaving information about each other's trains off their timetables. Nick Salmon wanted to travel from Leeds to Newcastle early one morning and consulted the Regional Railways TransPennine Express timetable. He found no obviously suitable through train starting around 7am. He had, however, vaguely heard of a 07.10 departure and rang the station which confirmed its existence. But why wasn't it in the timetable? 'Different train operating companies,' they told him.

Mr Salmon — who is no relation to Roger Salmon the franchising director — points out that the TransPennine timetable includes some InterCity trains but only those which appear to complement, rather than compete with, Regional Railways' services. Although the timetable is not comprehensive, it fails to explain this and does not say that there are other trains between, say, Leeds and Newcastle.

Many other readers have pointed out examples of 'invisible' trains which are run by InterCity but not mentioned, as BR does not want them to be used as local trains. For example, Sarah Hosking of Whitchurch says she often catches the 06.25 Euston to Crewe and wanted colleagues to join her at its first stop at Watford, but as this was not an advertised service in the timetable, she rang up to check whether the train did stop there. She was told that, yes, it stopped at Watford, but that InterCity did not want people to use the train to travel from Euston to Watford.

Damien Knight points out that just after 7 every evening, an almost empty train from Glasgow pulls into Gatwick Airport on its way to Brighton. He says: 'The direction board is blank. The tannoy announces "Do not join this train" and, virtually empty, it glides on nonstop to Brighton. Meanwhile, passengers for Brighton stand waiting for the often-delayed Thameslink service which, with its many intermediate stops, takes much longer.'

Response/comment: Howard Keal, press executive of Regional Railways North East, wrote in response to the section about the TransPennine services: 'To include all services (on pocket timetables) would have made the table too complex and unwieldy for a quick-to-use reference and it is made clear in the table that for parts of the route other trains are available. Helpful numbers for further details are also given. Active consideration is already being given to redesigning the current timetable to make it easier to use by splitting it up into different versions for the various markets it currently covers. Part of the change being investigated is to make the new separate tables more comprehensive for the section of the TransPennine route they cover by including InterCity services.' Mr Keal cannot resist pointing out that 'Regional Railways North East produce the only timetables in the country to be awarded Plain English Campaign's Crystal Mark for the clarity of the information given.'

Several readers commented that the 'Mad' column was being unfair in citing the other two examples in this item as they had nothing to do with privatisation. Martin Taylor of Guildford pointed out: 'Some longer-distance trains have for years made certain stops to pick up only or to set down only. In many cases this is a perfectly sensible rule. It would clearly be absurd for a Euston–northwest England train to become overcrowded because of local passengers travelling to Watford Junction.' However,

Mr Taylor agreed that the restriction on the InterCity train travelling between Gatwick and Brighton, prompted surely by the fact that it is operated by a rival company to Thameslink, 'seems quite unnecessary'. Indeed, it runs at a time when many business travellers are arriving back at Gatwick and it could quite easily be used to take them to the coast since, as Mr Knight points out, it normally has very few people on it.

'Hello. I've been standing here for at least half an hour and there's still no sign of the train to Brighton.'

11. So Railtrack is Being Privatised?

Railtrack, which owns all the bits of the railway that don't move, is being prepared for privatisation. Many readers have written in with examples of how Railtrack appears to be trying to maximise its revenue to boost the potential share price.

Ann Sainsbury of Blisland in Cornwall reports that from April 1995, car park charges of £1 per day at Bodmin Parkway are being levied for the first time. Ms Sainsbury points out that people park there for no other reason than to catch a train as the station is three miles away from the town itself. 'In fact,' she says, 'as buses here are almost non-existent and there is no pavement on the A38 leading to the station, there is virtually no alter-native to driving to Bodmin Parkway and leaving your car there.'

She says that many people travel to Plymouth each day to work or study and British Rail should be encouraging them to travel by train: 'Even for a lone commuter, it will be considerably cheaper to drive into Plymouth and anyone going to London for a few days will have to pay £1 each day they are away.'

But it is Railtrack which owns the

THIS STATION HAS BEEN AWARDED THIRD PRIZE IN THE CLEANLINESS AND TIDINESS COMPETITION

station, not the train operators. Ms Sainsbury points out that Railtrack has no vested interest in boosting train use, merely in increasing its own revenue. She says: 'It will just persuade more people to drive to work, resulting in loss of revenue to British Rail and more congestion on the roads.'

From Somerset comes another example of increases caused by Railtrack's need to raise money. Kay Barnard, a Liberal Democrat county councillor, says that Railtrack's greed is putting at risk the lives of schoolchildren by holding up the construction of a footpath between Lusty rail bridge and the river bridge at Bruton on the busy A359.

The path is to make the road safer for the large number of pedestrians, particularly schoolchildren, who use the road. But a small part of the path, around 20m by 1.8m, is under a railway arch and belongs to Railtrack. The county council's director of property services duly wrote to Railtrack expecting that the council would be charged a small token rent.

Back came a demand for £3,150 per year, which Ms Barnard calculated means an annual rent of £300,000 per acre. Ms Barnard says that a representative of Railtrack told the director at a meeting that £300,000 per acre was by no means the highest which the organisation was planning to charge for land.

Response: Other readers have pointed out that it is not Railtrack which lets out parts of stations or sets car park charges, but the train operating companies. However, the train operating companies all have to pay rents to Railtrack for the stations which they use, something which never happened in the past. Therefore, they are under pressure to raise revenue in all sorts of ways and increased car park charges are one of the few possible ways of doing this. Of course, ultimately it is counter-productive since it makes using the train more expensive relative to car journeys, and therefore many potential train passengers will be deterred. As Ms Sainsbury pointed out, it seems particularly ludicrous to levy charges for car parking at Parkway stations since the whole point of such stations is to attract car users on to the rail network. They are, too, built outside towns where land for car parking is cheap and therefore there is little justification on cost grounds for the charges.

Update/comment: Railtrack is being floated just as this book is being published. If anything illustrates the real motives behind the privatisation of the railways, it is the sale of Railtrack. Originally, privatisation was presented as a way of boosting competition on the railways and attracting private investment. Railtrack was supposed to be an afterthought, sold off after the whole franchising process had been completed. Then in 1994, the agenda changed and Railtrack was to be the flagship part of the privatisation, sold off before most of the franchises had been let. Since there was no plan to break it up or to make it compete — an impossibility anyway — Railtrack will be a monopoly supplier, entirely dependent on government subsidy. A leaked memo from the chancellor, Kenneth Clarke, in November 1994, gave the game away. The sale of Railtrack became an integral part of his budget plans in order to pave the way for tax cuts. It was Railtrack's attractiveness for sale and the fact that it would bring in a substantial sum for the government coffers which made its sale so imperative.

Railtrack takes great pride in the stations that it possesses and actively encourages competition amongst its station staff.

12. So You Want to Use Red Star?

Red Star, which was the subject of a failed privatisation attempt, is now withdrawing its service from many stations, as Lynne Curry found out. She complains that Red Star Parcels are no longer accepted at her local station, even though one of the selling points of the service was supposed to be its nationwide coverage. She tried to send a parcel recently, but was told she would have to go to Bristol 13 miles away.

On asking the reason for the reduction in service, she was told: 'The train company takes their bit and the station company theirs, and then there is so much for each parcel, so that it doesn't pay.' Of course, all these various companies used to be BR and indeed all of them are still in the public sector.

Ms Curry points out that the same staff member who used to pick up the parcels is still employed at the same station and the same trains run at virtually the same times. But the accounting mechanisms used to break down each component part of the service mean that it has ceased to be viable. And, as Ms Curry points out, 'more parcels will now have to go by road'.

Update/Comment: After two failed attempts, Red Star was eventually sold to a management buy-out team in late 1995 for £1. The minister involved in making this decision, John Watts, admitted that one consideration in deciding to proceed with the sale was that it could be carried out quickly if it went to the management buy-out team, despite the fact that other outside bidders had offered more money.

Red Star is another good example of how the break-up of the railway, in the name of efficiency, leads to results which are far less efficient than the original situation. Red Star was reasonably profitable until the early 1990s when the method of accounting was changed in order to identify the costs of the service. Therefore, the Red Star division of BR began to be charged for all kinds of costs which previously had been assumed to be part of the overall expense of running the railway. For example, it was charged rent for the use of parts of stations, and even had to pay for space on trains. This may be an accountants' Nirvana, but it makes little real economic sense. The real extra cost of a train carrying a few light parcels is virtually nil and the station space, usually bits of platform hither and thither, used by Red Star is mostly completely useless for any other purpose and therefore would be impossible to rent out to any other commercial outfit.

Yet, because of these new costs, the service became heavily loss-making, at least in pure accounting terms. In practice, nothing had changed. Therefore, when it came to selling it, the service had to be rationalised to as few outlets as possible, much reducing the use — and usefulness — of the Red Star concept.

The high cost of Red Star was pointed out by several readers who question whether it should be so expensive when the marginal cost of adding a package to a train is so small. John Stubbs wanted to send a 13kg package from Salisbury in Wiltshire to Ripley, Derbyshire, and was told it would cost £32.96. His local post office quoted £8.25, while Mr Stubbs said he could have delivered the package himself, using his OAP ticket and even taking a taxi from Derby to Ripley, for £32.50.

Service cuts are already biting. David Edgar says that when he rang the Red Star service at Birmingham, he was told that the service is available 24hr a day. However, a notice at the despatch and collection office — near another boasting a 24hr service — says the office is only open between 6.15 and 21.45 Monday to Friday, with shorter hours on Saturday and — since August 1995 — not at all on Sundays. He points out: 'So outside these hours, the service is available merely in the sense that the closed office with its fine logo and helpful notices is still physically there'.

And you say that the price of the parcel to Leeds is £12.50 and, for an extra £1.00, I can buy the company?

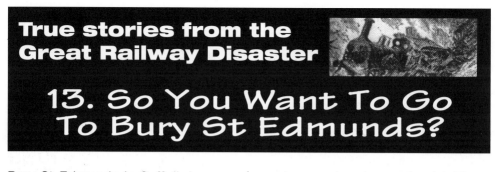
13. So You Want To Go To Bury St Edmunds?

Bury St Edmunds in Suffolk is on a cross-country line between Cambridge and Ipswich and can be reached from London by changing at either of those stations. The distance and time are roughly the same.

However, Martin Whitfield, a regular visitor to Bury St Edmunds, has discovered that the timetable at the station lists trains via Ipswich to London Liverpool Street, but does not mention services via Cambridge or Ely to London King's Cross, despite the fact that certain trains going that way are faster and offer better timings. He feels that as there are only a few trains per day, it might be imagined that all services would be advertised on the local timetable.

In fact, the relevant information is hard to come by in London, too. At Liverpool Street, timetables exist only for services via Ipswich. At King's Cross, no timetable whatsoever mentions the possibility of connecting trains to Bury St Edmunds.

Services between Bury St Edmunds, Ipswich and Liverpool Street are operated by Anglia, while services between Cambridge, Ely and King's Cross are operated by West Anglia Great Northern, a different train company. Both, of course, are still in the public sector and belong to British Rail, and neither is due to be franchised to the private sector until 1997 at the very earliest.

Mr Whitfield wrote to West Anglia Great Northern to ask why all trains were not listed. Patricia Timewell, the aptly-named customer relations officer, replied: 'We cannot advertise a connecting service from Bury St Edmunds to London via Cambridge as such a service does not exist. There are no guaranteed connecting services within West Anglia Great Northern, nor between ourselves and our fellow train operating companies.'

Yet, the BR timetable clearly shows that there are such connections. The train enquiry service in London continues to give full information on both alternatives, but those at Ipswich and Cambridge favour their own services. The operator at Ipswich, for example, said there was no train to Bury from London between 14.30 and 17.00 — both Anglia trains — despite the fact that the 15.15 and 16.43 from King's Cross both connect easily via Cambridge and are offered as available by enquiry staff in London.

None of this was surprising to Mrs Timewell. She wrote: 'There is limited space available at Cambridge station and we do, therefore, put primary importance on advising our travellers of the services offered by West Anglia Great Northern.'

She concluded: 'It must be taken into consideration that during the restructuring for privatisation, BR was split into separate companies. Consequently, we have no more jurisdiction over a fellow train operating company, such as Regional Railways, than we have over London Underground or any other public transport company.'

Response: Jonathan Denby, Anglia's PR, wrote: 'Our policy is that Anglia Railways stations and telephone enquiry bureaus (sic) provide the appropriate information for the journey being made, irrespective of whether it happens to be by our services or not.

Connections to Bury St Edmunds are prominently advertised ...

The Rail Regulator has raised guidelines about impartial retailing which we, and other operators, must adhere to. If mistakes are made or inaccurate information given, we will rectify the situation. We have asked West Anglia Great Northern to put Bury St Edmunds connections in their timetable.'

He concludes: 'We are quite clear that it is in the interests of both rail users and train operators for train operators to co-ordinate effectively.' He points out that Central Trains' Norwich to Peterborough service is included in the Guide to Anglia Railways 'since many of our customers use those services as well as Norwich to London InterCity services.'

Comment: This one is the hardy perennial of the 'Mad' column (see also, for example, Nos 21 and 33) and many rail users have sent in similar examples. One reader, K. L. Hall of Epping, Essex, decided to take the matter up with his local MP, Steven Norris who happens to be a junior transport minister. In the manner of these things, Mr Norris passed the letter on to his transport colleague, John Watts, who then wrote to Roger Salmon, the head of the Office of Passenger Rail Franchising, (OPRAF).

Jon Foster, the head of OPRAF's secretariat, eventually wrote back to Mr Norris stating, 'There is no reason why privatisation should lead to a lack of communication between operators or lack of co-ordination of their services. The co-ordination of rail services will be an important aspect of franchising, and the Franchising Director will, through franchise agreements, be encouraging co-operation between operators to preserve and promote arrangements which facilitate the making of journeys by more than one passenger service operator.' Mr Foster then makes an interesting point which addresses the whole dilemma of where competition is allowed to override the immediate interests of passengers: 'For instance, operators will be required to offer inter-available tickets where the Franchising Director believes that the benefits of doing so *will outweigh the likely benefits of price competition and service diversity* (author's italics)'.

Then Mr Foster addresses the issue of train information. He says: 'The provision of clear and prompt information to passengers will be another important condition that station and passenger service operators will be required to meet. All operators will be required to provide comprehensive and up-to-date information *about the services they offer* (author's italics) and to keep passengers well informed about any alterations or delays to services. Moreover, station operators will be required to provide impartial information about the services of all operators that use the station, and passenger service operators will be required to provide impartial information about other operators' services that interconnect with theirs.'

It is clear from the point in italics that there is no obligation on train operators to tell anyone about similar but rival services.

As Mr Hall points out in a rejoinder to Mr Norris, Mr Foster's letter 'doesn't and cannot answer the question, which was: "If operating companies wished to publish timetables for their own trains only, not those of other operators on the same routes, would the Government allow such a thing to happen?" ' Mr Norris replied 'No'. However, as Mr Whitfield's letter and many similar examples in the 'Mad' mailbag show, many stations — which, apart from a dozen or so major stations, are all run by a specific train operator and not by Railtrack — do not display full information about rival operators' services and many train operators publish timetables which omit other companies' trains.

A well-maintained diesel engine emits no fumes (allegedly).

'I'm sure a train must have been past here within the past six months.'

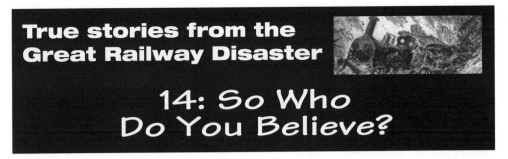

14: So Who Do You Believe?

The key thing rail travellers need — apart from the trains running on time — is accurate information. Tom Knight arrived at Manchester Piccadilly from London with only seconds to find out where his connection was due to depart from. He had to go to Chinley, in the Derbyshire Peak District, to address a meeting and his London service had arrived a little late.

Rushing up to a woman official in a smart new maroon uniform, he asked for the Chinley train. She consulted a computer and told him: 'It's leaving from platform 1 and you've got 30 seconds.' Mr Knight made it just in time to leap on board the train. But when the conductor arrived to check his ticket, he learned that he was heading for the south Manchester suburbs and not east to Chinley.

An angry Mr Knight had to get off at the next stop, take a train back to Piccadilly, then wait an hour for the next service. While kicking his heels at Piccadilly, he complained to a British Rail official about having been misinformed by the woman whom he was able to point out on another platform: 'Sorry, sir, you can't blame us,' said the man. 'We're Regional Railways, and she's InterCity.'

Of course, by the time Mr Knight had got to Chinley, he found he had missed the meeting. Worse, he found he was not entitled to compensation from either company. InterCity claimed that it was not responsible for that section of his journey, while Regional Railways said it did not have late running trains that day and therefore it, too, was not to blame.

Response: We wrote to both InterCity West Coast and Regional Railways North West, but neither responded.

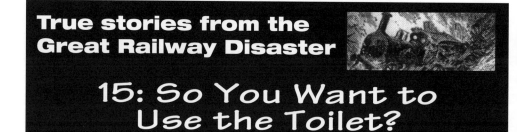
15: So You Want to Use the Toilet?

Trains on the West Coast main line which connect London with Wolverhampton, Manchester, Liverpool and Glasgow are currently serviced by depots at each of those locations. In preparing for privatisation, the West Coast main line management is considering closing the London depot at Wembley in the run-up to privatisation in order to save money,

with the consequent loss of 250 jobs.

There is, however, what could be called a 'sanitary' problem. In the course of the day's travel up and down the lines, toilets get blocked and are closed up by the guards to wait for overnight maintenance. At Wembley, there are facilities for toilets to be properly cleaned and, as it were, flushed through.

If the Wembley depot were to close, the trains would stay overnight on platforms at Euston station where there is no similar facility for a full cleansing and flushing service. And since the West Coast main line trains' toilets are the old-fashioned 'plop on the line' type without retention tanks, they must not, as every literate passenger who has ever used a train toilet knows, be flushed while trains are standing at stations.

Therefore, under the proposal to close the depot, the toilets would have to await repair until the next time the train is at the other end of the line. This is usually the following night, but sometimes, particularly if there are train cancellations, it could be several days ahead. Passengers, meanwhile, would find themselves with a diminishing number of toilets, especially as those that were in working order would be increasingly used and therefore more liable to be blocked up. There would also be an increasing risk that the blocked, swilling toilets would leak into the corridors. Not a pretty prospect.

Wembley, being at the end of the line, is, of course, one of the busiest depots, but the decision to earmark it for closure was taken by management on the basis that alternative employment for those made redundant would be easier to find in London than in the other cities.

Update: This may have been another victory for the 'Mad' column since InterCity West Coast abandoned its plans for this rationalisation soon after this column appeared. A spokeswoman said that the idea 'had only been at a preliminary stage'.

In a bid to raise its profile, one of the Train Operating Companies launches its new 'state of the art' livery.

16. So You Want to Use the Toilet? (Part 2)

Allan Horsfall has been campaigning for a long time to get toilets reinstated at Bolton station where the main facilities were closed three years ago because of vandalism and the lack of maintenance. He was within a whiff of success until the advent of the break-up of the railways in anticipation of privatisation. The Greater Manchester Passenger Transport Executive, which subsidises public transport services in and around Manchester, had been prepared to make a grant for improvements at Bolton station that included 'a new shelter, a chargeman's office and toilet facilities, including disabled and night facilities'. Although this had been delayed for a couple of years because of a shortage of funds, the PTE had hoped to proceed last year, but was unable to do so, according to a Mr Woolvin, its rail services manager, 'because of the changes in procedures and organisations in the run-up to privatisation'.

The problem for the PTE is that it has been warned that if it makes a grant to improve the station, leasing charges or track access charges to the train operators may then be increased by Railtrack to reflect the improvements made to the property. The PTE already pays substantial subsidies to support train services in the Manchester area and it does not want to pay more because of grants it has given to make those improvements.

As Mr Woolvin put it in a letter to Mr Horsfall, 'I am sure you realise it would be invidious if the investment of public money in funding improvements led to an increased demand for subsidy from the operators,' so until

the matter is sorted out, Boltonian rail passengers will just have to hold on a bit longer.

Meanwhile the *Daily Star* reports that BR has found a new role for the toilet roll. Passenger Chris Meek disputed a fare on an InterCity train between York and Leeds and the guard took down his details on toilet paper, claiming that he had no official notepaper because of cutbacks.

Update: Greater Manchester Passenger Transport Executive said in February 1996 that there was 'no change in the situation that gave rise to the particular issue' covered in this item. Gareth Mercer, press officer for the Executive, which is owned by the GMPT Authority, said: 'The Authority is still determined to protect any investment it makes, particularly with rail privatisation looming. The Authority does not wish to invest public money in a project only to see its investment sold off to the private sector and taken out of public use. The Authority is unwilling to make an investment and then see that investment used to increase a private company's profits at the expense of others, ie if the Authority invests in a station, it does not want to see Railtrack increasing its charges to operators as a result of those improved facilities'. (See also No 55 for a similar example.)

There is a wider row going on between the passenger transport executives which fund rail services in the main urban centres outside London and the Government over the way the subsidy is paid for. As a result of the new financial structure of the railways, the level of subsidy they need has approximately doubled because of the high cost of track access charges. Until April 1996, the Government gave a special Metropolitan Railway Grant to pay this extra, but from that date the extra money is being channelled to local authorities who will then have to hand it on to the passenger transport executives. This puts at risk the subsidy of rail services because, as the GMPTA points out, the expenditure will be in competition with housing, social services and education and there will be a temptation to cut back on transport spending. GMPTA has argued that the separate Metropolitan Railway Grant should be retained and, in fact, GMPTA has decided to withdraw from subsidising railway, forcing the franchising director to pick up the tab. The other passenger transport executives around the country have not taken this decision but rail privatisation has led to great uncertainty about their future ability to fund rail services in their areas.

Welcome to Bolton. Passengers ... sorry, customers ... are advised that the nearest toilet facilities can be found at Manchester Victoria. Intending users are advised to phone in advance as engineering works, particularly at weekends, may result in the temporary closure of these facilities ...'

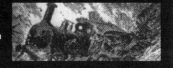

17. So Your Train Needs a Shunt?

Jim Nisbet of Edinburgh recently discovered that the railways may soon need the equivalent of the AA or the RAC. Last month, he was a passenger on a charter train which had to reverse at Sheffield station. The timing of the train allowed 15min for the locomotive to be uncoupled and a fresh one to be attached to the other end. For some reason, this simple operation took 40min and the train eventually left the station 25min late.

Mr Nisbet and his fellow passengers were then offered a bizarre explanation over the train's tannoy. The charter was being operated by Rail Express Systems, British Rail's mail trains division, but the shunter belonged to Regional Railways North East. The passengers were told that before the uncoupling and coupling could begin, the driver had to obtain an authorisation code from RES at Crewe to ensure that the £300 payment for this task would be made by RES to Regional Railways North East. Mr Nisbet adds: 'I am sure the fact that the station was managed by someone employed by yet another rail company, InterCity Midland Main Line, didn't help matters. The emphasis on accounting seems to be a far cry from the days when the prime objective was to get the train away on time.'

Response: Howard Keal, press executive of Regional Railways North East, replied to our enquiry by saying that it was impossible to find out exactly what happened on this occasion without more precise details, but that in general 'arrangements are made in advance to authorise shunting and to ensure the operation is carried out quickly and smoothly. Without being given a date, Regional Railways North East is unable to establish what may or may not have happened in the case quoted.'

Update: This tale is by no means unique. Talking to a station worker at Llandudno Junction in the autumn of 1995, the author heard an almost identical story. A loco-hauled train had broken down near the station, but although there was an unused freight locomotive at sidings nearby, a locomotive belonging to the same train operating company had to be sent all the way from Chester, delaying passengers by over an hour, to relieve the stricken train because using the freight locomotive would have cost the train operator money.

Robin Bevis of Ivybridge in Devon related how an InterCity Cross Country train from Liverpool to Plymouth broke down at Bristol Parkway. Passengers were told there would be a delay of at least an hour while a replacement engine was sought, but while chatting to the conductor on the train, his daughter was told that the delay would have been considerably less if they had been allowed, as in the past, to use the nearest spare locomotive. But it belonged to another rail company, Great Western, and their service could not use it. Mr Bevis comments: 'So the accountants say "no" to using another company's loco and the passengers are delayed for over an hour. And yet the Government tells us that privatisation will benefit passengers. Truth seems to be shunted up a siding and left to rust as far as this dogmatic policy is concerned.'

There have also been enormous problems with train charters and many operators have gone out of business, claiming that prices had gone up by so much that it was impossible to operate any more trains (See No 49). Much of the blame was put on RES, which was given the monopoly on supplying locomotives and staff to charter train operators, and was eventually privatised in December 1995 to a consortium led by the US freight company Wisconsin Central.

Comment: The response is nevertheless interesting in that it seems to accept that this sort of thing could happen. The co-ordination required between the different train companies for trains which travel through many areas is difficult to achieve and there are bound to be times when the paperwork has been lost in the bureaucracy or the 'arrangements' have not been made through some oversight.

'£500 or the train doesn't move!'

18: So You Want to Go to Birmingham Slowly?

A bedraggled reader, Iona McTaggart, complains of a tortuous journey from London to Birmingham on a train without refreshments or air conditioning. Her misery was, in fact, a result of Railtrack's obsession with competition.

InterCity runs trains every half-hour throughout the day from London to Birmingham with weekday journeys taking, typically, just under an hour and three quarters. There are also regular slow trains between the two cities which take almost an hour longer because they are really intended for passengers using the intermediate local stations.

For many years, therefore, BR has operated a kind of subterfuge in the interests of its passengers. It kept secret the fact that these slow trains run all the way through to Birmingham. They were, instead, advertised as terminating at Northampton, in order not to attract passengers seeking to go to Birmingham as it would always be slower for them to use the stopping service, even if they had just missed a fast train.

Enter Railtrack with its emphasis on competition. It now runs Euston station, as it has kept direct control of a few large main line stations rather than leasing them out to train operators. Railtrack is insisting that the trains are shown as Birmingham trains on the departure board because they are run by North London Railways, a potential competitor of InterCity West Coast, and Railtrack claims it must be even-handed between the operators at its stations. The fares are, actually, identical and therefore there is no possible benefit for travellers wishing to go to Birmingham to take the slow train all the way, unless they have a fear of speed or particularly like the view from the train.

Response: Railtrack defended this change vigorously in its response. Kate Smyth, the press officer, wrote: 'Public information systems exist to inform the public. Railtrack endeavours to give the travelling public the fullest information possible in order to allow them to make up their own minds what to do, a view adopted by Which? magazine. The North London Railways services terminate at Birmingham, so they are displayed as terminating at Birmingham. As with the West Coast services, the noticeboard also displays all the stations at which the train stops, whether there are any restaurant/buffet facilities and whether it's an InterCity train or not, so that passengers can decided which service they want. The InterCity service to Birmingham is half-hourly.'

Update: In January 1996, slow trains were still being advertised as going through to Birmingham and Railtrack says this is the right policy. Kate Smyth, its spokeswoman, said: 'You've got to be pretty stupid not to realise which trains are slow and which are fast'.

Comment: This item was actually submitted by a very high official within BR headquarters, showing the anger and frustration of many senior managers in the rail industry at the ludicrous procedures which are being introduced in the name of competition and efficiency. Railtrack's response is slightly economical with the truth. The

'Good afternoon. Welcome to Euston. The fast train to Birmingham New Street, with full buffet service, will depart from platform seven. The slightly slower service, which may (or may not) have a trolley refreshment service, will depart from platform two. The very slow service, with no refreshment facilities at all, will depart from platform ten. Please note that the following tickets are available as follows.... Confused, you will be!'

underlying reason for this initiative in displaying these trains as going through to Birmingham is to encourage competition.

Certainly, Railtrack's position is not logical. It is clearly misleading for people not familiar with the railways, such as foreign tourists, to show the information in this way without specifying that travellers to Birmingham should take an InterCity service. But Railtrack clearly does not dare to do that through fear of the legal consequences. If it were seen to favour one service in relation to another, the matter could be referred to the regulator or even the courts.

19: So You Want to Buy a Timetable?

Graham Larkbey of Hornsey, north London, recently asked at Victoria station's ticket office for the free supplement which is always produced by BR to provide corrections and amendments to the main timetable.

The enquiry clerk shook his head: he could not supply one because the concession to sell timetables at Victoria — and at several other large stations — has been given to WH Smith. The shop is also supposed to hand out the supplements but retail outlets are not used to handing out free goods, so they are often not available to passengers. Mr Larkbey found that the WH Smith at Victoria was out of stock and did not know when new supplies were coming in.

Even train operators now find it is harder to get hold of copies of the national timetable. Operators such as Network SouthCentral at Victoria now have to buy the timetables from the British Rail Board which will not provide them on a sale or return basis. In the new commercial world of railways, they dare not risk losing money by over-ordering but therefore may find themselves short of timetables for their own purposes.

Mr Larkbey also points out that it is now harder to get information from displays at railway stations: 'Previously, when divisions of BR wanted to improve the advertising of services at their stations, they just stuck up a few more display boards. Now, every additional display board has to be agreed by Railtrack, the station landlords, and each extra one is liable to lead to an increase in the amount of rent paid by the train operator to Railtrack.' Therefore, there is a financial disincentive for operators to provide extra information, and with space constrained in this way, they are even more likely to provide information only about their own services.

Response: We wrote to Railtrack headquarters for its comments, but we received no reply.

Update: This item preceded the great timetable disaster of autumn 1995. Railtrack took over the publication of the timetable for the first time from BR. Because part of the culture of the 'new railway' is that if BR did it one way, it must be wrong and therefore it has to be done another way, Railtrack asked a computer company to devise a new programme for timetable production. The company failed to deliver on time and Railtrack was forced to employ a second set of consultants, which also did not manage to produce the software quickly enough. Railtrack was then left, belatedly, to use the old BR software but did not allow itself enough time to produce an accurate timetable. The result was that there were so many errors that a supplement of over 300 pages had to be produced immediately, and a second supplement quickly followed, which meant that passengers had to consult three different sources to ensure they got accurate information. Even some MPs found themselves misled.

Eventually, Railtrack was forced to publish an entirely new timetable for the second part of the winter 1995/6, the first time that this has ever happened.

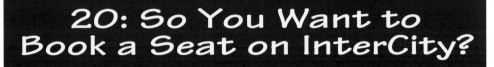

20: So You Want to Book a Seat on InterCity?

InterCity, one of BR's three main operating divisions, used to run most of Britain's long-distance train services and published a detailed guide. Now these services have been handed over to eight different train operating companies. The InterCity name survives for advertising purposes, but the organisation no longer exists and so neither does its joint service for selling tickets by telephone, as David Davies of Wakefield discovered.

It used to be possible to book any of these services via a freephone number and tickets would be posted, or alternatively, passengers could telephone major stations and reserve tickets to be collected.

The InterCity guide to services is still published, but the 'Rail Direct Telesales' page has disappeared. So has the list of major stations. Now each operating company has its own booking system with different details and varying arrangements such as opening hours and number of days allowed for delivery of tickets.

For example, Midland has a freephone number but does not allow collection from main stations and requires five days for delivery, while East Coast lists only its main stations, with different opening times, and says seven days must be allowed for delivery or otherwise tickets must be collected.

ScotRail lists its main stations, but only for sleeper bookings (as those are the only trains south of the border which it operates) and each station has different opening times (or you can collect, but not from Dundee).

And so on and so on...

Update: This type of complexity which passengers now face is bound to increase as InterCity's various lines become privatised. InterCity fought a long and unsuccessful battle to be allowed to continue as a single entity after privatisation. It was successful, at least, in ensuring that the InterCity brand name survived, but in the long term, if all the parts of InterCity are privatised to different companies, this arrangement is bound to be jeopardised and will probably eventually disappear.

Great Western Trains was, in fact, one of the first of the three franchises to be privatised. The contract was won by the management buy-out team, but initially the preferred bidder was a completely unknown group of former railway managers and business people called Resurgence Railways. However, Resurgence was unable to find the necessary financial backing and the management buy-out team was awarded the franchise in December 1995.

InterCity East Coast, Gatwick Express and Midland Main Line are also early candidates for privatisation, while other services have been handed over to ScotRail, Anglia and Cross Country. InterCity West Coast was to have been sold off early, but the sale has been delayed because of the problems in devising a scheme for the new franchisee to refurbish the line and trains.

A guide to InterCity services was still available free in February 1996 from an address in Derby and advertises a freephone number, 0800 450450, through which bookings can be made. Indeed, Terence Smith of Biggleswade in Bedfordshire reports that he has found the service very efficient, booking trips involving three train operating companies and sending him the tickets which arrived the following day.

Nevertheless, for people complaining, the booklet is more complicated than its predecessor, listing seven addresses depending on what train was involved. And the future of the InterCity brand is dependent on continued co-operation between the seven companies once they are privatised.

'Rail Direct Sales. I am afraid that this service has been withdrawn. Please refer to your local coach operator for the best through ticketing service.'

21. So You Want an Accurate Timetable For Your Route?

The new BR timetable which came into force at the end of May 1995 seems to have given the various train operating companies a great opportunity to restrict the amount of information offered on 'rival' train services when publishing their local timetables. The pocket timetable for trains heading north out of Newcastle, for example, used to include the service between Newcastle and Berwick showing both InterCity and Regional Railways trains. Now, however, Regional Railways North East has issued the timetable showing trains only as far as Chathill, which is the northern limit of its area, even though all the trains go on to Berwick.

Reg French of the Selby District Rail Users' Group points out that Regional Railways North East has also now unaccountably missed out the stopping trains between Selby and Leeds on its Hull to Leeds timetable. Mr French suspects that this is because the slower trains are run with the help of a grant from the West Yorkshire Passenger Transport Executive, while the other trains are paid for entirely by RR.

Andy Brabin of Wandsworth Friends of the Earth has had a long struggle to obtain timetables for all the trains leaving Clapham Junction. There are three companies running services there: South West Trains, Network SouthCentral and North London Railways. Mr Brabin reports: 'South West Trains, which operates the ticket office, had its timetables available. However, SouthCentral and North London timetables are nowhere to be seen.'

And according to Dr Paul Baker of Bournemouth, South West Trains' timetable for the Bournemouth to Southampton service no longer details trains between Bournemouth and Gatwick operated by SouthCentral or those between Bournemouth and Manchester or Edinburgh run by InterCity Cross Country. Instead, it lists only the services run by South West Trains.

Response: Mr French took up the matter of the Selby and Leeds service with Regional Railways North East who said that including all the trains was confusing to passengers. Mr French asked them how passengers could be made aware of the stopping service and he was told: 'They should refer to the West Yorkshire Metro Timetable.' Mr French says this contains 96 pages. Eventually, a notice was displayed at Selby station to try to clarify the position.

Regional Railways North East responded to our request for clarification with the following: 'All trains do not go to Berwick — as is suggested in the column — and Regional Railways North East no longer includes the stop in its pocket timetables because we no longer call there. We continue to produce pocket timetables for the services between Newcastle and Chathill in which we include the InterCity trains calling at the stations we both serve, including Alnmouth and Morpeth.'

The response on the Selby to Leeds service remained much the same as told to Mr French. Regional Railways North East said: 'Changes were made to the Hull–Leeds pocket timetable as there was concern that the previous

'If you hang on for a moment, Sir, I'm just printing out the full timetable for your train.'

version was too involved and a more easy to follow format was needed. The Selby–Leeds details were of no interest to the majority of users for whom the timetable was intended. The challenge was to provide a simpler version while making sure that the needs of Selby–Leeds travellers were still met. A separate timetable shows Selby–Leeds services, so these were taken out of the main pocket timetable and a note included in the front cover to alert people to the change. It also gives a number to call for information.'

Update: The situation at Clapham Junction remains the same. Several months after this item was published, the 'Mad' column was still receiving complaints about the lack of availability of information on trains other than those run by South West Trains at the station.

Comment: This whole book could have been filled with similar examples sent in by readers. While, in individual cases, train companies may be making these decisions for sensible reasons, there is no doubt that the general thrust of many of them is to stop people using rival companies' trains. For example, arriving at Gatwick Airport just past midnight one cold day in January 1996 and needing to take a train to London, The author picked up the Gatwick Express leaflet while waiting for his baggage to come through. It gave all the information on its wonderful service and gave the time of the last train as 23.50. In fact, there are hourly trains throughout the night operated by Network SouthCentral and there is another leaflet available which shows this service. Of course, that makes no mention of the Gatwick Express trains...

22. So You Want to Use a Rival's Train?

'Basingstoke. This is Basingstoke. The train on Platform 3 does not stop here except for passengers who booked three days ago. Those customers wishing to use the train are advised that seats are available on the train running next Tuesday.'

The new rail companies being prepared for privatisation are going to extreme lengths to keep rivals' passengers from boarding their trains. Not opening the doors would appear to be the tactic chosen by Regional Railways, South Wales and West, on its Carmarthen to Waterloo route.

When the train stops at Basingstoke, the doors are kept locked, as Martin Whitfield from Bristol discovered recently, in order to prevent ticket holders of South West Trains getting on to board the service for London. Mr Whitfield was forced to go on to Woking and return by another train to Basingstoke where staff said the Regional Railways train was a 'setting down' service only.

Passengers on the platform are told they aren't allowed to join the train and according to Mr Whitfield must wait 20min for a South West Trains services.

Ticketing arrangements on the Carmarthen–Waterloo service are also byzantine. Passengers must book in advance. This can be up to 16.00 on the day before departure if you collect the tickets, or five days before if you ask for them to be sent by post.

However, travellers between certain stations don't need a reservation if they want to do the journey on a day when one of 10 'counted space' reservations are available. Asked about the problem of getting information about the train at Bristol where enquiry staff are employed by InterCity Great Western, a South Wales and West employee said: 'We have difficulty in getting the message across to sell our train, when they are trying to sell their own services at the same time.'

Response: We received a lengthy explanation from Chris Gibb, manager of Western Cross Country for Regional Railways South Wales and West. He wrote: 'The 06.00 Carmarthen –Waterloo train involved in this incident now regularly loads around 100 passengers (capacity 134) and all our service loadings are increasing. Between five and ten passengers now usually alight at Basingstoke, leaving insufficient seats on the train for the number of passengers that may be waiting on the platform. We have not had a single complaint about problems of alighting at Basingstoke since this incident. We have had more letters of compliment concerning our Waterloo services than criticism. The service is very popular and growing in popularity. Many passengers travel from West Wilts to London, between places like Bristol and Woking and for journeys to connect into Eurostar.

'From time to time the train will no doubt run full in the immediate future and we are determined to ensure, like an airliner or long-distance coach, that everyone is seated in comfort. Most passengers happily accept this 'constraint' in return for the excellant (sic) value for money these services represent, and avoiding the need to change trains or cross London. The service has been extensively advertised and most of our passengers have found out about the service from advertising or from a recommendation from another user.

'With all these trains there are South West Trains services minutes before or after — not 20min as stated by Mr Whitfield. For the 06.00 Carmarthen–Waterloo, departing Basingstoke at 10.23, there are Basingstoke–Waterloo express trains at 10.15 and 10.31.'

Mr Gibb implies it is not rivalry with SWT that dictates the policy, by adding that there is often co-operation between the two companies: 'In the event of disruption, we liaise closely with SWT to jointly provide the best possible service, as we jointly share in many of the revenue flows involved. For example, on 11 November 1995, the 19.05 (SWT) Waterloo–Salisbury failed at Waterloo and on request from SWT the 19.18 Waterloo–Carmarthen called to pick up and set down at Clapham Junction, and additionally to set down at Salisbury. Exceptionally, on this day, the train had passengers standing for some of the journey.'

Mr Gibb also suggests that stopping only to set down or pick up passengers has been a 'common railway practice throughout the world for many years. Trains have called as such at Watford Junction, Motherwell, Hamburg Dammtor and Versailles-Chantiers to pick up/set down for many years and famous trains such as the Bernina Express, Puerta Del Sol, East-West Express, and Rheingold have all called in this way for a variety of reasons.'

Mr Gibb concludes by saying that the seat reservation arrangements have improved and 'are now available up to the time of train departures on these services'.

Comment: The other examples cited by Mr Gibb tend to relate to long-distance trains stopping at suburban stations (See No 10) and which therefore do not want to take local passengers for short hops. It is quite unusual to have a train such as the one involved not picking up passengers still some way from its destination.

The main point, however, is that South West Trains would undoubtedly resist any attempt by Regional Railways South Wales and West to directly duplicate one of its services, the Basingstoke to London service, and would probably ask the rail regulator to intervene. The regulator has decided that to allow such open access to the railways would make it impossible to let out franchises, as the franchisees would always be at risk from rival operators coming in and cherry-picking the most lucrative services. Therefore, it is very unlikely he would sanction the right of Regional Railways South Wales and West to stop at Basingstoke, even though this would provide a useful additional service for some passengers. In order to avoid a difficult argument therefore, Mr Gibb has bowed to the inevitable by decreeing that his train will not stop at Basingstoke, even though he admits that it is never full, except in the event of other trains being cancelled.

23. So What's The Fare For the Bicycle?

Terence Warneford of Malvern overheard the following conversation at Malvern Link station. A boy wanted to take his bike down the line to Colwall. He asked Gary, the station-man, about the fare:

'It's 70p single, 90p return.'

'Can I take my bike on the train?' asked the young boy.

Gary, a helpful and knowledgeable railman who has worked on the railways for donkeys years, according to Mr Warneford, replied: 'On some trains you can, on others you can only if there's room.'

'How much does it cost?'

'On the green ones, it doesn't cost anything, but it's up to the guard to let you on if there's room. On the blue and white ones, it costs £3 per journey.'

The boy was bemused: 'So it would be 90p for me and £6 for the bike.'

'That's right. Sorry, son.'

'I'll get my dad to take me in the car,' said the lad, and trooped off to find his father.

The green trains are run by Centro which operates trains in the West Midlands area with the help of considerable subsidies from the local authorities. The blue and white trains are run by Thames Trains, one of BR's 25 train operating companies.

Mr Warneford explains that the poor boy, now lost to the train system for ever perhaps, would have to find out which train was coming first because Thames operates a penalty fares system, while Centro does not. He would also have to consult two timetable to make sure he wasn't taking his bike without a ticket on a train where one was required. Alternatively, he might have wasted £6 by buying a ticket for his bike when it would have been carried free.

Response/update: Paul Dobbie, the media and external relations manager, for Centro, agrees that the wealth of companies now providing rail services can cause difficulties for the humble passenger. He writes that this item 'does illustrate how confusing it can be for travellers to have so many organisations involved in running rail services'.

He then goes on to explain, but not necessarily to enlighten: 'The main point to emphasise is that the service in question, while sometimes served by Centro-subsidised rolling stock (the 'green ones') is in fact not a Centro-sponsored service. The position is that Regional Railways Central, which runs trains on our behalf, can use Centro-subsidised rolling stock on cross-boundary services or when it is not required for Centro-sponsored services.'

According to Mr Dobbie, Centro introduced a £10 penalty fare system across the West Midlands in June 1995, some time after the incident in this item occurred, bringing it in line with Thames.

In an effort to be helpful, Mr Dobbie enclosed further information from a Peter Sargant, of Centro's rail services section but this will only leave readers more confused.

Mr Sargant accepted that the policy of rail carriage had been causing confusion and that as a result Regional Railways has 'decided to conform with Centro's free carriage policy on cross-boundary routes'. However, this has not necessarily simplified matters because 'this has therefore caused inconsistency with other operators, such as with Thames Trains. With regards to this particular story, Regional Railways, Thames and InterCity Great Western all operate on this route. Thames and Great Western both operate the £3 fee for bikes.'

The timetable does not offer a way out of the dilemma faced by the boy and his bicycle. Mr Sargant explains that 'the Centro/RR timetable for the route shows all services run, regardless of operator. However, we do not show the operator by individual train and so a passenger would have to enquire for that information.'

Mr Sargant is clearly aware of the absurdity of the situation, as he ends with the wry comment: 'While this story is entirely outside the Centro area, and therefore not in our domain, it shows how Centro's benevolent attitude to the carriage of cycles has given passengers at Malvern Link the opportunity to take their bikes for free on some services which would not have been possible otherwise!' (His exclamation mark, not mine.)

Lou Tate of the external affairs department of Thames Trains added a bit more confusion by saying that bikes cannot be taken at all at certain times: 'As far as Thames Trains is concerned, bicycles cannot be taken on trains that arrive at London Paddington station between the hours of 07.45 and 09.45 Mondays to Fridays, or to depart between 16.30 and 18.30 from Paddington. Bicycles can be taken on our trains at any other time and there is no charge.'

Comment: This does appear to be somewhat of a victory for the 'Mad' column, but only a very partial one in that the policy of free carriage of bicycles has been extended to all cross-boundary journeys. However, it does not seem to help the boy as his journey is entirely outside the Centro area and the lad would still have had to pay £3 for his bike if he got on the wrong train. As Mr Sargant explains, it is terribly difficult to find out in advance which train is due first since the timetable does not show which

operator is running a particular train. And if you 'have to enquire for that information', how do you do so at an unstaffed station?

It is also bizarre that Thames is prepared to take bikes free, while other companies charge. Surely, given that cycling is being encouraged by the Government as good for health and good for transport, should not the franchise director or regulator intervene and make other companies carry them for free?

'Next time, I think I'll go by car!'

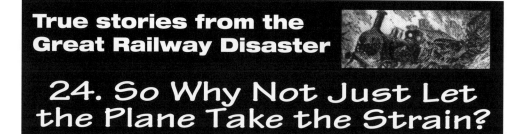

24. So Why Not Just Let the Plane Take the Strain?

Tom Wilkie and his family wanted to travel by train to Wurzburg in Germany, so he went down to Waterloo railway station, the departure point for the Eurostar trains on which he intended to travel for the first leg of the journey.

At the 'Travelcentre' on the main concourse, they said: 'Not us mate, we're British Rail' and directed him downstairs to the Eurostar ticket office. At one of the counters marked 'Eurostar and beyond', Dr Wilkie asked the price of a ticket to Wurzburg. Try as he might, the incredibly polite and helpful young man behind the counter could get neither of his two computers to give him any information about Wurzburg.

One computer belongs to Eurostar, he explained, and contains all the information about getting to Eurostar's destinations in Paris and Brussels. The other belongs to British Rail International, and contains all the information about other continental rail stations. They don't talk to each other.

Dr Wilkie's home computer is linked to a service called Compuserve, which provides detailed information about all British Rail and continental train departures, including arrival and departure times. The night before his visit to Waterloo, Dr Wilkie had taken only a few seconds to consult the machine, which planned his route for him.

Dr Wilkie offered the young man the information that a trip to Wurzburg involves changing trains at Cologne: 'That explains it,' the young man said, with all the enthusiasm of Archimedes jumping out of the bath. 'There is no connection to Eurostar.'

Dr Wilkie protested: 'But we want to go to Brussels on Eurostar and then link up with the continental rail service.'

But no. Because the journey involves changing at Cologne, it is not a direct service from Brussels and therefore tickets must be bought through British Rail International, the young man explained. Eurostar cannot access the service details or sell tickets because it is a rival company to British Rail International and they are both about to be privatised in completely different ways.

As a parting thought, the ticketless Dr Wilkie enquired about taking a car on the train through the tunnel: 'We're Eurostar, sir. That's Le Shuttle, which is Eurotunnel and they're a different company.' As Dr Wilkie turned to leave, the man whispered, 'Take the plane, sir, it's cheaper.'

Update: There has been no improvement in this situation. Eurostar, which is part owned by European Passenger Services, has deliberately been created as a completely separate entity from British Rail. Therefore, there is very little link between the two and their computers appear to be incompatible. In a radio interview in January 1996 at which this specific example was raised, John Watts, the railways minister said: 'This is nothing to do with privatisation. BR International has never had a presence at Waterloo station and the opening of Waterloo International providing Eurostar is a new development and EPS have acknowledged that your passenger should have been offered a through ticket from Eurostar through to the nearest German destination which they serve.'

Asked if BR International is not allowed to sell tickets at Waterloo to protect EPS's share of the market, Mr Watts said: 'It's not a matter of not being allowed to sell tickets at Waterloo. The nationalised structure of BR has not operated at Waterloo. It's always operated at Victoria. As we develop private sector services, and Eurostar is privatised as part of the Channel Tunnel Rail Link competition, the private owners will be looking for opportunities to develop services and maybe that will be to offer tickets to a wider range of European destinations.'

As the book went to press, EPS was on the point of being handed over to the winning consortium to build the link, London & Continental, which includes Richard Branson's Virgin group.

Dr Wilkie ended up struggling to Wurzburg by train with his family, but, flew back from Munich, a deeply disappointed man.

'In all honesty, sir, I would suggest that you take a cab to Edinburgh airport, take the Shuttle to Heathrow and change if you want to get to Germany.'

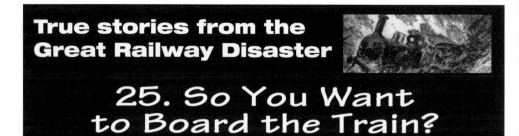
25. So You Want to Board the Train?

Regular users of the Gospel Oak to Barking line in north London know it to be one of the most notoriously late, slow and unreliable routes in London. Elizabeth Blunt discovered the line's new initiative to meet train time schedules when trying to travel home from Gospel Oak station. The company's plan seems to be not to stop at intermediate stations along the route.

On a recent Saturday afternoon, she was waiting to catch the 16.51 which pulled into the station 10min late. The many waiting passengers eagerly converged on its carriages. The train sat there for a further 11min and then the guard told passengers who were not intending to travel all the way to Barking that they must leave the train. His explanation was that as the train was now running 20min late, to catch up lost time it would be running through all the intermediate stations without stopping.

Mrs Blunt and her fellow passengers were not pleased: 'The anger of the train-load of people left behind on the platform must have been nothing compared with the bewildered rage of people left behind at intermediate stations as they watched their long-awaited train trundle straight past them.'

To Mrs Blunt, the initiative seems clear. 'The North London Line has realised that if you don't carry passengers, then you don't have to waste time stopping at stations to let them off.' She thinks this is a classic example of the often desperate measures adopted by several of the new train operating companies in a bid to cut down lateness to meet Passenger's Charter targets. The targets are based only on arrival times at the final destination and therefore cutting out intermediate stops enables them to be met. With privatisation in the offing, managements are desperate to ensure that they meet the targets.

Response: Graham Bashford, Corporate Affairs manager of North London Railways wrote: 'On a line where there is a 30min interval service, a delay to one train of 20min means that the following train is only 10min behind. Depending on the prevailing situation, it is sometimes to the benefit of the majority of customers that the late running train reaches its destination as quickly as possible in order to start its next trip on time instead of all services being late for the rest of the day. The additional 10min delay for those waiting for this particular train is understandably frustrating, but the decision to run a train fast to its destination will only be taken if a larger number of people waiting for services later in the day will benefit.

Comment: The Passenger's Charter has been the subject of much criticism. An investigation by *Rail* magazine, in conjunction with the BBC's *Here and Now* programme, found that time had been added to many scheduled journeys in order to enable the train companies to meet their Passenger's Charter targets. The article quoted Ivor Warburton, the head of InterCity West Coast, saying: 'The allowances have been increased by a minute or two to give our customers consistency and reliability.' In response to questioning, he went on: 'The Charter produces published standards and if we are to achieve those standards then we need to review the schedules and ensure that we reduce the variation so that we can produce an offer — the timetable — that we can deliver. I accept that a few minutes have been inserted into some of the schedules to ensure that we can more consistently deliver on time.' This was confirmed by Barry Doe, a timetable analyst, who says that there was a gradual increase in journey times throughout the network between 1989 and 1992, and a few more random additions since then.

As Mrs Blunt points out, the Charter figures relate only to the time at the final destination. They also are normally calculated only on certain trains, often at peaks, failing to give the full picture.

'I must remember to stop at Upper Holloway. I must remember to stop at Upper Holloway. I must remember to stop ...'

26. So You Want To Go To Etchingham?

Etchingham station in Sussex. The lack of a train is evidence of the veracity of the information provided by Waterloo. Now if only our photographer had waited until a train from Victoria was due ...

Brendan Hughes often travels between Brussels, where he lives, and his parents' home in Etchingham, East Sussex. He takes the Eurostar to Waterloo International where he transfers to Waterloo East and catches the Hastings train to Etchingham.

On a recent occasion, Mr Hughes, arriving at Waterloo International at 21.00, crossed to the main concourse and looked at the timetables to check when the Hastings train was departing.

Strangely, when he checked under E, Etchingham was missing.

The ticket office clerk explained that due to privatisation of the lines, Mr Hughes could not reach Etchingham from Waterloo but would have to go to Victoria via Clapham Junction and take a train from there. Mr Hughes did so, taking two trains to reach Victoria station which is only a couple of miles away by bus. But at Victoria he found the only Hastings train was via Gatwick, totally out of his way, and the Tunbridge Wells trains appeared only to run at peak times. Instead Mr Hughes took a train for Redhill, via Clapham Junction, and changed there for Tonbridge. He finally arrived at Etchingham after changing once more at Tunbridge Wells. It had taken him two and a half hours to make a journey that normally could be done in 45min.

On his return journey, Mr Hughes was not taking any chances. He phoned Tonbridge where he learnt that the London–Hastings line was operating normally. He was also given the explanation for his earlier tour of the suburban rail network. He was told that while most trains through Waterloo East are run by South Eastern trains, those from the main Waterloo station are run by South West Trains. Each is unwilling or unable to sell tickets for its rival. Customers for Waterloo East services must use a special booth on the concourse but Mr Hughes did not know this and went to the wrong ticket office, which directed him on his merry-go-round.

Response: Keith Merritt of South West Trains is surprised at the difficulties encountered by Mr Hughes. He wrote: 'Etchingham can be found in Table 207 in the Great Britain Passenger Timetable and is served by trains on the Cannon Street and Charing Cross to Hastings route. Services departing from Charing Cross stop at Waterloo East which is where Mr Hughes will be able to board his train crossing over from Waterloo International. Having checked with the Waterloo ticket office manager before committing myself, I would like to confirm that Waterloo main line ticket office will quite happily sell Mr Hughes a ticket to Etchingham valid for travel on services departing from Waterloo East.'

Mr Merritt concludes: 'I hope that I have managed to reassure you and Mr Hughes that travel to Etchingham is not as difficult as first envisaged.'

Comment: This type of error by ticket clerks has been reported by many readers. The crux of the matter is that the separation of services into so many companies, often operating out of the same station, is bound to lead to such absurdities. Eventually, it is very likely that there will be entirely separate ticket booths, just as at airports there are different sales desks for every airline.

27. So You Want Your Charter Train to Stop at the Stations?

The new structure of the railways has created enormous problems for rail charters as costs have soared for the companies running the excursions. They are charged what seem to be very high access charges by Railtrack and also have to pay high rates for train crews provided by Res, the company which runs the mail trains and which has been given the monopoly on providing staff for charters.

JMC Rail Tours used to run rail charters from Whitby to Middlesbrough along the attractive Esk Valley line and beyond. This acted as a big attraction for people along the line which has 16 stops, enabling many people in the local villages to join the trains.

No more. For each stop, JMC is being charged £52 by Railtrack, making the charter uneconomical. Linda Lloyd, a director of JMC, commented: 'We used to charge £19.50 for the journey, but this has become unrealistic and we now have put the fare up to £29.50.'

As a result, the charter service is now 'in hibernation' while Ms Lloyd, backed by her local MP and many local people, tries to lobby Railtrack to change the system. She says the trains provided a much-needed boost to the local economy: 'When we took out trains into Whitby, we were bringing 500 people into the town who would use the local fish and chip cafés and the souvenir shops. Now they've lost that business.'

She points out that Railtrack, too, is a loser. No other trains used the line on Sundays and whether her trains stopped or not could not possibly cost Railtrack any extra money, she said. At least there is some consolation: the Esk Valley line has just received European money to appoint a publicity officer to try to boost its use.

Response: It took a long wild goose chase around the industry to find out who was responsible for these charges. Kate Smyth at Railtrack, the first port of call, wrote back saying 'Railtrack is not responsible for making any charges for stopping at stations not managed by Railtrack. In the case of the JMC Rail Tours charter from Whitby to Middlesbrough, Railtrack would agree a track access charge with the train operating company running the charter. Station stops would be covered by station access charges which in this case would be agreed between Res (the mail train company, now privatised, which provides locomotives and staff to charter firms) and Regional Railways North East which leases the stations from Railtrack.'

So, we approached Regional Railways North East which, after much difficulty and delay, came up with the following answer from Howard Keal, its press officer, who wrote: 'We do charge a small amount for station access but these figures in no way relate to the sums that have been suggested by the charter operator. Calling at an unstaffed station costs £5.17, staffed stations £20.66.

'Where a train is longer than the platforms, we insist on providing a supervisor to ensure safety standards are met. The supervisor sees that people get on and off the train in the correct, safe, place. The charge for a full day would be £123.12 Mondays to

Saturdays, and £146.24 on Sundays, making it possible to stop at all 17 stations on the route. Other costs would be shunting at £6.34 an hour Mondays to Saturdays, and £10.85 on Sundays.

'All the above charges would be plus VAT, and an 11.9% *(why is it not 12%?)* service charge.'

Mr Keal points out that these charges reflect the real cost to train operating companies. He concludes: 'The way the industry is now structured means charter operators have to pick up the true cost of the services with which they are provided. Hidden subsidies were previously provided by BR which absorbed costs that must now be passed on.'

'Mad' was unable to get back to JMC to check the figures because no one answered its telephone. Perhaps it had gone out of business, a victim of rail privatisation. The sums quoted by JMC were, however, similar to those asked of other charter firms at the time by Res and it may be that this was the origin of the figures. However, Res refused to discuss a specific case due to 'commercial confidentiality', the expression that has become the catch phrase of the industry since privatisation has arrived. (See also No 49 for a discussion of other problems faced by charter firms.)

'I'd just like to say thank you for stopping our train at this station. Much appreciated!'

28. So You Want to Take the Ghost Train?

Kenneth Hope-Jones has been a regular traveller between Redhill and London, via East Croydon and relies heavily on his Network SouthCentral pocket timetable, which has recently been reissued.

Recently, while he was waiting at East Croydon to travel out to Redhill, a train for Redhill and Tonbridge was shown on the monitor screen. It was even announced on the loudspeaker and duly arrived at the time shown on the screen.

When Mr Hope-Jones referred to his timetable, he found the service did not seem to exist and yet there was the train appearing, not surprisingly, to be completely empty. Not believing his good luck, Mr Hope-Jones approached a nearby guard and asked about the mysterious train.

'Ah,' the guard replied to his questioning, 'that's not one of our trains, so we don't put it on our timetables. It's another rail company that runs the train.' He went on to say that the station had only recently begun even to recognise the existence of the train by announcing its arrival: 'We used to just slip it out quietly without letting on it was going to stop at Redhill,' the guard replied with a mischievous smile.

A now-perplexed Mr Hope-Jones enquired about the frequency of the trains and was even more astonished to discover that it was a 'regular service'. He is not the only one to be confused by these trains. Soon after the service was introduce, in May, a local councillor, Godfrey Horne, was astonished to see passengers being barred from joining the train at East Croydon by Network SouthCentral officials. The reason was that there was a doubt over whether Network SouthCentral ticket holders would be able to use the train which is operated by South Eastern Trains. This has now been sorted out, but far be it for one company to advertise the other's services!

Update/Response: Another great victory for the 'Mad' column. Simon Eden, press officer for Network SouthCentral, responded to our complaint by writing: 'From June 1996 of this year, Network SouthCentral will fully advertise this service by:
- Including it in all of its timetables
- By making station announcements
- By displaying it on station TV screens.'

Comment: Why has it taken so long? The service was introduced in May 1995.

Railtrack's state-of-the-art monitoring station designed to record the operation of 'ghost' trains; unfortunately, nothing seems to be visible.

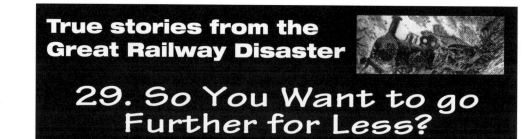

29. So You Want to go Further for Less?

Wanting a return ticket for travel from London to Newcastle upon Tyne, Mike Dutchie found that it was cheaper to travel further. Mr Dutchie of central London needed to get to Newcastle on an InterCity train before lunchtime to attend a family wedding on a weekday, so he opted for the 0.800 morning train, at a cost of £124. Yet, after arriving at Newcastle, the train continues to Edinburgh and the return fare to the Scottish capital is only £72 from King's Cross.

The reason, as far as British Rail is

concerned, is simple: even though you might be on the same train, the Newcastle trip is classified as a business service, while the Edinburgh one is a leisure service. A Saver fare is available on the Edinburgh journey, but not on the Newcastle one.

Mr Dutchie warns that business travellers to Newcastle should not try to save money by buying an Edinburgh ticket and getting off on Tyneside because they may not be allowed back on the train at Newcastle without paying a hefty supplement.

Update: See No 61 for a discussion of similar examples including the case of the Sevenoaks children being charged more for travelling a shorter distance.

Comment: This is not really about privatisation, but about commercialisation of the railways. The InterCity example demonstrates how fares aimed at business travellers have been pushed up in order to maximise revenue, a policy that is bound to create the sort of anomalies highlighted by Mr Dutchie.

Left: 'Well, you did inquire about the cheapest fares available...'

Above: The devil and the deep blue sea — passengers threatened with dire consequences if they travel without tickets but with no means of actually being able to purchase them.

30. So You Used the Wrong Ticket Machine?

Morris Graham went on a day trip from London to Brighton with a group of friends. On the way back, on the 23.00 train from the south coast, the passengers for London were told to change at Gatwick and board the Gatwick Express. When the Gatwick Express shuttle left the station, Mr Graham and his friends were asked to show their tickets. Then, the group was bemused to discover that some, but not all of them, were charged a £1.40 excess fare.

They tried to find out why. All had paid £11.90 that morning at Victoria for their day returns. However, some of Mr Graham's pals had bought their tickets from one of the booths in the station. A second lot, those who happened to have the right change, had bought them from ticket machines. And a third group, the unlucky ones, bought them from a different ticket booth. It was only when the inspector on the Gatwick Express train checked the tickets that Mr Graham noticed that some of the return tickets were marked 'London Brit Rail not Gatwick Express' while the others were marked simply 'London Brit Rail'.

When Mr Graham queried why some of his friends were being charged £1.40 extra for the same journey as him, the inspector said: 'The discrepancy should be taken up with the company which sold you the tickets.'

'Needless to say,' adds Mr Graham, 'it is not possible to tell which company you are purchasing tickets from at Victoria and no one had warned any of the travellers that their tickets would not be valid on some trains. The tickets do not indicate which company has sold them.

Response: Simon Eden, press desk manager of Network South Central, admitted there had been an error by the computer and wrote: 'Mr Graham's friends, the unlucky ones that is, should not have been surcharged. It was a programming error — which was soon identified and corrected — that led to the ticket machine issuing them a ticket stating "not Gatwick Express". This means they were entitled to a refund and Network SouthCentral would not have hesitated in giving them a refund under these circumstances.'

Mr Eden then anticipates our objections by asking 'But how can you claim a refund when the machine is anonymous?'

'This is no longer the case. Each ticket machine must now display the name of the appropriate train company. So, should a similar error occur, they would know who to contact.'

'With all the new restrictions, the new standard ticket will be about this long.'

31. So You Want the Cheapest Ticket to Birmingham?

Werner Ullah needed to travel from London to Birmingham for a morning meeting and rang British Rail enquiries to be told that the fare would be £54 return, as no cheap tickets were available for travel before 11.00. However, he remembered that he had once travelled to Birmingham using the Chiltern line from Marylebone, rather than InterCity services from Euston.

He rang British Rail again, but it said it could only issue tickets for InterCity services and eventually he had to go to Marylebone to find out the full details. There he discovered that Chiltern was doing a special £19 return deal, any time, any day, any train, and was told that there was a train which would get him there in time for his meeting, even though the journey takes a bit longer since it has more stops than InterCity. Even without the special deal, the cost would only have been £25.

Mr Ullah duly saved himself £35 by travelling via Marylebone, but asks: 'What can be the justification for such a price differential, even taking into account the speed of either service? The Tories seem keen to turn us into a nation of train fare spotters.'

He says that it was only because he had previously travelled on Chiltern that he knew about the service to Birmingham: 'The absurdity is that unless I had travelled on the Chiltern line before, I would not know that it was an option and British Rail neither tells people about it nor allows you to book through them.' He adds that the Chiltern line 'should also do much more to publicise itself, and to offer telephone booking'.

Response: InterCity West Coast insisted that Mr Ullah would now be informed of the Marylebone route. George Reynolds, its public affairs manager, wrote: 'There is a formal obligation on train operating companies to quote the lowest appropriate fare for a journey. The formal impartial retailing obligation came into effect in October 1995 and all retail staff, supervisors and managers are aware of the obligation and how it should be discharged.' See No 59 for several more examples of the lowest fare not being quoted, despite the obligation referred to by Mr Reynolds.

Comment: The British Rail office which Werner Ullah rang was probably run by InterCity. The Chiltern line was at the time probably prevented from marketing itself too aggressively because of the wrath it would face from InterCity while both of them are still in the public sector.

Railtrack's solution to the problem of passengers' requests for information — the unstaffed advice bureau. Guaranteed to ensure that all requests for information are handled equitably, whatever the Train Operating Company concerned.

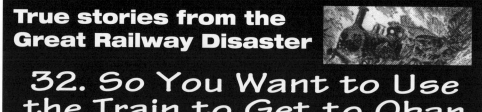

True stories from the Great Railway Disaster

32. So You Want to Use the Train to Get to Oban For a Cruise?

Hebridean Island Cruises used to encourage its passengers to buy 'all-inclusive rail packages' to reach its ship, the MV *Hebridean Princess*, at Oban on Scotland's west coast. No longer. It has just sent out a letter to its customers warning them not to use the railway any longer.

The company says that as 'British Rail are rearranging their procedures in

SORRY MADAM WE CAN'T THROUGH-PLATFORM-TICKET YOU TO SEE ALL THE TIMETABLES

preparation for privatisation, regrettably everything we hear at this time leads us to believe that, in the short term, there is nothing on offer other than an increasing array of difficulties for travellers'.

Two particular problems have arisen. It used to be possible for those buying Hebridean Island's all-inclusive rail packages to travel across London in time to get the 10.00 train from King's Cross to Glasgow. This is no longer possible if they are coming from south of London as these tickets are not now accepted in the morning rush hour by the local train operators. This is a consequence of the division of BR into 25 separate train operating companies which apply different rules on accepting cheap tickets.

Secondly, Hebridean Island says that BR will no longer allow a refund of the cost of the rail travel, or permit it to issue revised tickets, unless, according to BR, 'the reason for cancellation involves cancellation of the whole package'. This lack of flexibility makes the purchase of rail tickets risky.

The company's letter says that 'since it became clear that the privatisation of BR will, at least in the short term, provide travellers with an inferior service, we can only recommend that whenever possible guests should consider the option of travel by other services'.

There's no such problem with the airlines since Hebridean Island Cruises says: 'During the rail strike last year, a large number of our guests used the all-inclusive Tartan Air Service' we offer from Heathrow and they found it very straightforward and convenient.'

The letter adds: 'I regret these further deficiencies in the rail system but you will appreciate we have little power to make changes, although we are making strong representations.'

Clearly, as Noel Harvey who contributed this item put it: 'There will be more cars on the road to Oban in future.'

Who needs a boat for a cruise — ScotRail launches its own brand of 'sail by rail' trips.

Jim Grozier found himself at Three Bridges station in West Sussex recently and sought to find out what trains were available for London. On platform 3, he was confronted with a poster simply headed 'Train Times' which actually shows all Network SouthCentral trains together with those operated by Thameslink, but only as far as London Bridge. Further Thameslink destinations such as Luton and Bedford are left out and there is no explanatory note.

Over on platform 2, there is another timetable board headed 'The Trains' which shows all the Thameslink services — although, of course, they are served from platform three — including those to Luton and Bedford, but omits all Network SouthCentral services. Again this is not explained.

Common sense appears to prevail on platform 5, as the two timetables appear side by side, but in the ticket hall there is no information on Thameslink, only on Network SouthCentral trains under a heading bearing that company's logo.

Mr Grozier, who lives in Brighton, is worried that this timetable separation will soon reach the south coast where there are six train companies operating. He suggests that at Brighton if each company had a separate timetable and separate weekend engineering works posters, 'hapless travellers would have to consult 12 documents before taking a train. Now that would be a boost for the motor industry,' Mr Grozier comments.

Response: John Watts, the railways minister, attempted to give an explanation of the rules governing information at stations on the Radio 4 *You and Yours* programme in January 1996. He said: 'The regulator is making it a condition that operators offer impartial information about all the services that are available from the stations which they operate.

'They are required to provide information and it is my belief that failure to deliver the information that is required is not a deliberate attempt to prevent passengers finding out what would be best value for them, it is because the information is based upon very thick books and whether a particular booking clerk can give a passenger the full information he might require depends on his degree of knowledge and skill and his ability to find the thing in a book.'

Comment: So Mr Watts thinks it's all down to ticket clerks not being able to read a timetable. In fact, this issue of 'competing' train companies not providing information or not trying to make connections with other companies undoubtedly outweighs any other in terms of the number of letters in the 'Mad' mailbag. See No 13 above for a discussion of the issues and the promises made by the Office of Passenger Rail Franchising.

Update: Jim Grozier kindly returned to Three Bridges in February 1996, six months after the original item appeared, to check whether the situation had improved. He reported: 'There do seem to be more timetables, though the improvement is only marginal. There are now Thameslink timetables on all platforms except

Platform 1, but not in the ticket hall. There has been no change in the Network South Central timetables, not even the addition of a footnote to explain their limited "catchment area". There is still no cross-referencing anywhere. '

As for Brighton, he says the Network South Central timetable actually includes major Thameslink destinations, but not smaller ones. He adds: 'There is a separate Thameslink timetable, Regional Railways also has its own, but as yet there are no timetables for InterCity and South West Trains.'

He points out that at Gatwick Airport, an all inclusive timetable, under a NSC heading, is displayed which includes Thameslink, Thames, South Eastern and Gatwick Express trains, which he says, 'is a model of what can be done'.

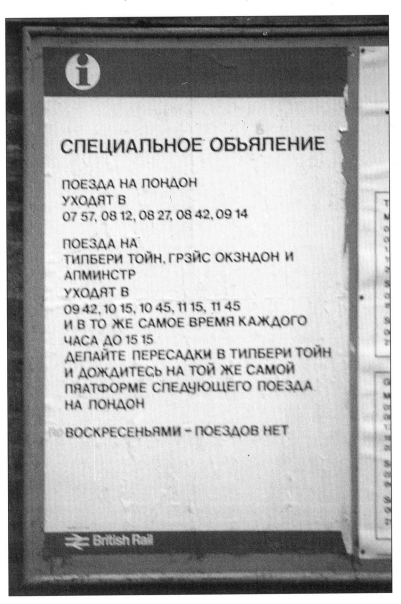

In their new spirit of openness, the Train Operating Companies have adopted a new format for their poster campaigns. Everything should now be clear ...

34: So Competition is a Good Thing?

Passengers at Denmark Hill in south London may be confused as to why every half hour they have two trains to central London within 3min of each other and then none for 28min. And coming the other way, those who have taken a train from Victoria and change at Denmark Hill have a very slim chance of catching the Blackfriars–Sevenoaks service as it is scheduled to depart 1min later. As Graham Larkbey, secretary of the South London Link Travellers' Association put it: 'Some of the time you can just catch it by sprinting along the platform, but most of the time you just get the chance to see it pull out of the station.'

The story goes back some years. For a long time, Mr Larkbey's group campaigned to have the peak-hours-only service along the Peckham Rye–Victoria corridor extended to run during the day and eventually a few years ago they succeeded.

That service is run by Network SouthCentral, but South Eastern, a rival company, spotted what it thought was a market gap and launched its own Victoria–Peckham Rye–Lewisham–Dartford service.

While Mr Larkbey and his members were pleased to see the new service, he was worried that it affected NSC's Victoria–London Bridge via Denmark Hill service, especially as South Eastern's trains do not call at so many intermediate stops. Mr Larkbey's worry is that the South Eastern service will cream off passengers from the Network SouthCentral trains putting that service at risk and many passengers, particularly those at intermediate stations, will find themselves worse off. Mr Larkbey was

concerned, too, that 'Peckham Rye and Denmark Hill both have this uneven service pattern with two Victoria trains within minutes of each other followed by a long gap — 28min during the day and 58min in the late evening'.

Mr Larkbey has also fought a long battle to ensure that the South Eastern trains are advertised at Denmark Hill which is operated by Network SouthCentral. He says: 'Eventually, they put up a joint timetable, but they don't put up the promotional material which South Eastern puts out to try to boost usage of their trains.'

Response/Update: Unhappy about South Eastern's refusal to retime its trains, Mr Larkbey wrote to the Rail Regulator, John Swift, the man appointed to look after the interests of passengers in such disputes. Mr Swift's reply was unhelpful. He wrote: 'I have a duty, amongst other things, to exercise my functions in the manner I consider best fitted to protect the interests of rail users. However, I have no statutory power to require BR, or any of its main train operating companies, to maintain or provide particular services.' Mr Swift points out that 'the eventual decision on the minimum level of service to be provided by each franchisee is that of the Franchising Director'. Mr Larkbey responds: 'Faced with this response, one might ask what is the Rail Regulator for?'

Mr Larkbey has continued to try to press South Eastern to retime its trains. He says: 'I accept that Network SouthCentral may find it difficult to retime their trains because of congestion at Victoria, but I feel South Eastern could try better but just aren't bothered. I feel that if both trains were run by the same company, they would make more effort to co-ordinate them and come up with a solution to this ridiculous state of affairs.'

Comment: Mr Swift's 'amongst other things' is an interesting little phrase. It refers to the fact that he also has a duty to promote competition, which at times seems to conflict with his duty towards passengers, and therefore he would be very reluctant to enter into such a dispute.

'Ah, well. Only another twenty-seven minutes to wait.'

35. So You Want to Use the Eurostar Special?

Several readers have written to complain about the trains which connect with the international Eurostar trains at Waterloo.

Joan Tate was waiting at Wolverhampton for a service to Euston. She describes how 'a long train of first class carriages drew up and was announced as going to Waterloo. No one got on or off the train as it was totally empty. Cheered, as I was going to south London anyhow, I asked if I could get on this train.' The following conversation ensued:

'No, madam, or you will be charged for a ticket from Manchester to Paris'

'But there's no one on it?'

'No, madam, but those are the rules.'

The train pulled out, majestic and empty, and Mrs Tate got on the InterCity shuttle to Euston. As she travels regularly to south London, she asked if it were possible to buy tickets in future for the ghost train.

'How can I buy a ticket from Wolverhampton to Waterloo and travel by that train?' she asked the InterCity West Coast conductor.

'That's not our business, madam. It's a Eurotunnel train and you can get tickets only from them.' (In fact, it's Eurostar but everyone's confused about that, including British Rail employees.)

'Where from?'

'I'm afraid I don't know, madam, but it's a separate company.'

'I know, but if I want to buy a ticket, where do I get it from?'

'I don't know, madam, we are only InterCity and we are not told.'

Mrs Tate, clearly an indomitable character, enquired again on the journey back and was given the same story.

'But this is insane,' she said, suggesting that they could well add a carriage or two for the peasants from the Shrewsbury/Wolverhampton area 'if they want the Manchester–Paris passengers, who seem to be non-existent, not to be contaminated.'

'Yes, but that's not our business, madam. We are InterCity. That train is nearly always as good as empty.'

'So they don't want us on it, or our money. That's mad...'

'You said it madam, not me.'

Mrs Tate then recounted the story to the station-master at Wolverhampton — 'or whatever he's called now' — who told her: 'Those people you talked to, they're InterCity and they tell me nothing. I'm Regional Railways.' At which point Mrs Tate gave up.

Professor Vince Gardiner of Wimbledon in London has had a similar experience. Standing on the platform at Rugby seeking to go home, he found that two trains were due in the next few minutes. The 10.21 was shown as a through train to Waterloo which would avoid a tube connection through London and arrives at 11.46. The second, the 10.23, is scheduled to arrive at Euston at 11.36 but means getting to Waterloo by tube at around 12.10. He says the Waterloo train never has more than 20–30 passengers but the Euston one is always full and often has people standing. But like Mrs Tate, Mr Gardiner was not allowed on.

A cutting from the *Edinburgh Evening News* sent in by John Stevenson of Edinburgh outlines the difficulties in even getting on one of these Eurostar connection services. It reports that customers must first go to the continental booking office at Waverley station, run by InterCity East Coast, which does not open until 09.00, half an hour after the Eurostar train leaves on its way to Waterloo. The train has been virtually empty and has not been advertised. Bill Ure, the secretary of the Scottish Rail Users' Consultative Committee, is quoted as saying: 'This is just plain daft.'

Richard Hargreaves of Skipton, North Yorks, actually wanted to use the train and found it hard to find. He got off the Eurostar at Waterloo only to find no sign of the train for Leeds on the main departures board, even though it was due to depart in 10min. He wrote: 'Finally, I spotted an InterCity train at a platform in the far corner of the station and, though there was no information on the board above the entry to the platform to say where it was going, it turned out to be the right train.'

He complained to an official to ask why the train was not mentioned on the board and was told: 'The main Waterloo station (as opposed to the neighbouring International Station) would not be able to give out information about it.' Presumably this is because non-Eurostar passengers might actually want to use the train and would find out that they could not.

Mr Hargreaves comments: 'Typical of the kind of nonsense we read in your column and a singularly unhelpful way to welcome passengers who want to travel on to destinations off the East Coast line on this otherwise admirable service.'

Update: Many of these Eurostar connecting trains have continued to operate with amazingly few people on them. Readers report being one of only a handful on a full length train, and only 30 people were on the much-hailed first train from Edinburgh in July 1995. The trains were introduced as a result of a ministerial promise at the time the Channel Tunnel legislation was passing through Parliament to appease northern MPs who wanted to ensure that the regions were connected directly with the Channel Tunnel. Eventually, direct trains will connect various points in Europe with the British regions beyond London.

Response: European Passenger Services, the British part of the organisation which runs the Eurostar trains and which is being privatised as part of the deal to build the Channel Tunnel Rail Link, says that it does not want to allow ordinary passengers on to these trains because 'it would create expectations that they are to be a permanent service'. In fact, EPS says, the trains will be withdrawn once direct trains go through the tunnel to destinations beyond London.

Comment: EPS's explanation is only part of the picture as both commercial and security considerations lie behind this bizarre state of affairs. The problem is that the direct trains which carry on through to the Continent will not be able to be used for passengers on purely domestic journeys. This is because there are fears that passengers getting off would pose a security threat since they would be able to leave baggage with bombs on the train timed to blow up under the Channel Tunnel. This is despite the fact that railways around Europe run international trains, even in long tunnels through the Alps, without such constraints and it is an instance of security considerations being completely over the top. After all, cross-channel ferries carry unaccompanied goods all the time.

EPS's reasoning is somewhat flawed, as many train services are introduced and later withdrawn after a couple of years. What they didn't say is that these trains would be in competition with existing services run by the various InterCity companies which would object if EPS were creaming off some of their passengers for domestic services.

Danger
Do not touch the
live rail

Prenez garde au
rail éléctrique
danger de mort

Gefahr!
Nicht die
Stromschiene
berühren

Pericolo
Terza rotaia
corrente alta
tensione

Passengers must
not cross the line

Défense de
traverser les voies

Reisende dürfen
nicht das Gleis
überschreiten

Vietato ai
passeggeri
attraversare
i binari

36. So You Want to Get Lost Property Back?

Amid the disruption a couple of weeks ago when InterCity West Coast services ground to a halt because of power failure near Northampton (incidentally, trapping the author for two hours on his way to give a lecture in Coventry) George Wright left his bag on a train.

Mr Wright, travelling north from London, had had to leap off a train at Milton Keynes very quickly because, contrary to what he had been told at Euston, the driver said that the train's next stop was Crewe, rather than his intended destination of Lichfield where he was due to stay a few days. The bag was left on the train and before Mr Wright realised what had happened, the train had departed on its way to Glasgow.

Next day, he tracked the bag down to Glasgow Central station. Railtrack at Lichfield said there would be a £1.50 charge, which Mr Wright quite accepted, but when he asked if Railtrack could send the bag down to the Lost Property at Euston, the station-master said that this was no longer possible.

In the 'old days', as the station-master put it, this would have been possible, but now Railtrack would have to send it by Red Star at a charge of £22 plus 80p per kilo. Mr Wright comments: 'I should stress that the staff at Glasgow to whom I spoke several times were most apologetic about the situation. One said he wished he could just put it on a train for me, but wasn't allowed to because of the fragmentation of BR.'

Nearly a week later, Mr Wright, by this time in dire need of clean clothes, explained why the recalcitrant luggage had still not being returned: 'I can't get the bag because before Railtrack will release it to Red Star, they have to be in receipt of my £1.50. Now they will only accept cheques or cash and that takes time to get to them. On the other hand, Red Star will only accept payment by Visa or Access and I'm having to sort it out.'

Response: In answer to our letter, Railtrack's press officer, Kate Smyth, wrote: 'This is correct.'

Passengers using Queen's Road station in Walthamstow, east London, have long complained about its darkness at night. Relief seemed to be at hand when Railtrack began installing new lights earlier this year. But it was not to be.

According to Steve Foulger, of the local rail users' group, only half the station has had new lights installed. And, unfortunately, the trains, which consist of only two carriages, use the other part of the station where there is still very poor lighting.

Just to make sure that no passengers benefit from the new floodlighting, Railtrack has erected big barriers preventing people getting into the brightly-lit section and blocking access to the equally well-lit and potentially useful staircase that leads to Walthamstow Central station.

North London Lines, which runs the trains serving the station, says it knows nothing about the lights and rents only the part of the platform it uses from Railtrack. And Mr Foulger says: 'Railtrack just never answers any letters. They won't explain why we can't use that part of the station.'

Response: Railtrack had rather more to say about this than the previous item (see No 36). In a detailed note, Kate Smyth explains that the lighting has been provided along a disused part of the platform at Walthamstow Queen's Road because it is 'used as a staff walking route' which, she says, is a requirement under Health and Safety Executive regulations. She adds: 'It is not suitable for use by passengers and has never been used by passengers.'

On the point about the link between the two stations, she writes: 'A footpath link between the two stations for passenger use was an objective of the British Rail Board and the local authority prior to 1 April 1994 (when Railtrack was created) and Railtrack has taken this on.' But she explains that neither BR nor Railtrack has ever owned the land, which is intended for new housing, and 'Railtrack is discussing with the developers the possibility of them providing the footpath link as part of the development.'

Comment: All very well, but it does seem odd that the staff get lighting for their bit of platform, while the passengers have to struggle through in the dark.

Lamp — for the use of Railtrack staff only. Passengers should make their own arrangements for illumination.

89

38. So That's Why the Motorways are Taking the (S)Train?

The sight of locomotives being hauled slowly and perilously along motorways is becoming more frequent since the break-up of the railways. No fewer than a dozen readers sent in local newspaper cuttings or their own accounts of a recent move of an InterCity 125 locomotive from Plymouth. The stricken locomotive, named *The National Trust*, was being taken 250 miles for a refit at Crewe, but rather than having another locomotive tow the engine on the rails, it was being sent by lorry on a journey taking three days.

The reason, of course, is that Railtrack charges so much for access to the rail network that it is cheaper for the repairers, ABB, to transport the train by road, irrespective of the congestion and danger this causes to other road users. One reader who sent in the Plymouth cutting, Stephen Gale of Brixham, suggested that Railtrack should be renamed 'Surrealtrack'.

Other readers have also spotted trains on motorways. During the summer, Alan Pugh of Llandudno in fact became one of the world's leading motorway trainspotters one weekend when he saw two low-loaders carrying both carriages of a two-coach diesel unit along the M6 near Stoke, causing chaotic traffic conditions. He comments: 'Perhaps it's all a plot to make people use the trains.'

ScotRail also decided two send two three-coach electric units from Glasgow to ABB's Derby workshop by lorry. It was quoted a price of between £20,000 and £30,000 per train to travel on the railway, including the cost of renting a special locomotive and paying Railtrack for the access charges. It found that this was 20% more than the cost of sending the two coaches, which had been damaged by flooding, to Derby by road.

ScotRail also pointed out that under the old system, the cost of moving the trains by rail would have been absorbed by the whole system, while now it will have to be met from passenger income. And because of the break-up of the railways, it was easier administratively for ScotRail to ring up an individual road haulier, rather than having to deal with all the different parts of the rail network involved in such an exercise.

Response: ABB told the 'Mad' column that it does still use rail quite often for transporting locomotives, but it depended on the precise nature of the journey, the condition of the train and the relative costs. The ubiquitous Kate Smyth (see, for example, Nos 36 and 37) was quoted in the *Plymouth Evening Herald*, which ran the story under the headline 'Plain Loco', as saying: 'I can't comment on this case without all the details. Charging people to use the track is how we make money.'

Comment: There is a much bigger issue involved here than merely the ridiculous sight of trains on motorways. This example is a reflection of how railway costs are borne directly by the railways and can easily be quantified, while road costs are hidden and cannot be identified so easily. On the one hand, the train operating companies are saving money, at least for themselves, but on the other hand society is paying a heavy price. All those drivers who have to slow down to crawl behind these behemoths belching slowly through the English countryside are having to fork out extra money for petrol. They are, too, wasting time, which can be translated into money. (The major part of the 'benefits' in the calculations used when the Government assesses whether a road should be built is in the form of similar tiny time savings by drivers using the new road compared with the old road.) The *Plymouth Evening Herald* pointed out that police escorts from Cheshire, Staffordshire, the West Midlands, Hereford and Worcester, Gloucestershire, Avon and Somerset, and Devon and Cornwall would all have to help the lorry through at taxpayers' expense. And the Highways Agency and local authorities who maintain the roads will find that the surface deteriorates more quickly as these heavy vehicles crawl over them. Indeed, the effect on road surfaces increases exponentially as the weight from an axle rises and therefore these very heavy vehicles will cause considerable damage. Yet, all that is hidden while it is possible to work out exactly how much it costs to send these locomotives by rail. While this has always been the case to some extent — rail investment, for example, has always counted as government spending, while the roads programme has been seen as investment — this example shows how transport economics are becoming even more distorted by rail privatisation.

The train now arriving at platform three is coming by road ...

39. So You Want a New Station?

Rail privatisation was supposed to encourage a more intensive use of the railways, but Chris Wright of the Oxon and Bucks Rail Action Committee has found precisely the opposite.

Oxfordshire County Council has long supported the idea of reopening a station at Kidlington on the line between Oxford and Banbury which it was estimated would attract 350 passengers per day and reduce the number of local car journeys.

The station was originally costed at around £500,000, of which the country would have had to provide half. However, now that Railtrack has taken over from British Rail, the cost of the scheme has escalated to £850,000 because, according to Mr Wright, it needs to make a high rate of return on its investments. He says: 'In the new system, everyone wants their cut. It makes everything more expensive.'

Moreover, Thames Trains, the local train operator, had originally promised to pay part of the cost. But now that it is being prepared for privatisation, and may not win the franchise to operate trains locally, it says it cannot provide any grant towards the cost of the station, leaving Oxfordshire to apply to the Government for extra grant. Mr Wright points out that this poses a big test for the Government's transport policy: 'Last year only four new stations were authorised by the Department of Transport. What chances are there in the Government's transport lottery?'

Update: In February 1996, Dick Helling, Oxfordshire's public transport officer, reckoned that any possible starting date for the station was receding further into the future. He was still in negotiation with Railtrack but further issues of complexity had arisen. Whereas in the past, British Rail used to agree to take on the whole contract, with financial support from the council, Railtrack may in future only want to do part of the work — the section involving safety on the railway which it is legally obliged to do. This means that the council would have to contract out the rest, and the various contractors would then have to co-ordinate, causing extra delay and expense.

'At the moment' said an exasperated sounding Mr Helling, 'We've given Railtrack a form with lots of boxes on it to tick and they are trying to identify which bits they have to do and which bits we can contract out.'

He reckons that one reason why the price of building new stations has gone up so dramatically is that whereas BR used not to include all its staff costs for designing and drawing up the scheme — since these people were employed by the railway anyway and there was no real extra cost — Railtrack counts every penny.

Mr Helling also confirmed that Thames Trains was not going to put up any money because of its imminent franchising.

Comment: This example prompted others — see No 50 which raises yet more complex issues — and it shows that the new system of accounting and subsidy within the railway has increased the cost of providing new services. Because all parts of the railway are only looking after their own patch and only consider whether a particular innovation is profitable for them, any new services or stations become uneconomic. In this new money-oriented system, there is no way of including the social benefits — such as reducing the amount of cars on the road — in the equation when assessing a scheme. Moreover, as we have seen, the direct costs have escalated making it more difficult for public bodies to invest in such schemes.

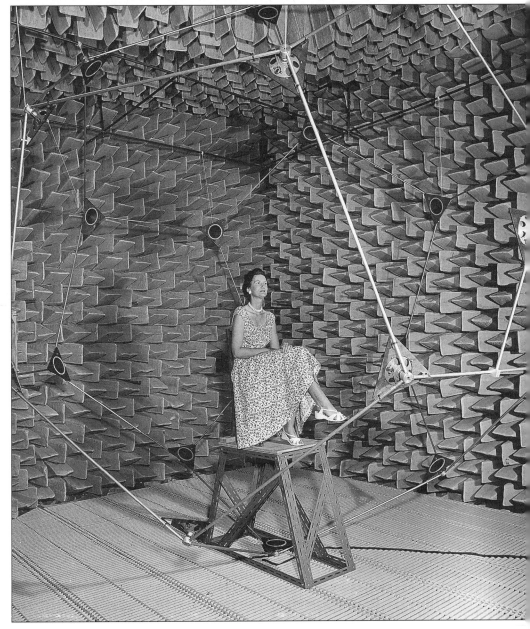

In order to get round the costs involved in opening a new station, Railtrack announce the introduction of the concept of 'virtual reality' railways. A satisfied customer thinks that she has safely arrived at Kidlington.

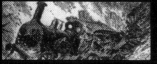
40. So You Think We Care if You Missed Your Last Train?

David Wilkins had a madder journey than most on his way from Sheffield to his home village of Tisbury in Wiltshire which necessitated changes at Bristol and Salisbury. The train between these two stations was delayed for 80min, making Mr Wilkins miss the last train from Salisbury to Tisbury. He had been assured at Bristol that he would be put into a taxi in Salisbury at British Rail's expense, but when he finally reached the station at 23.00, the duty manager said he was unable to help because missing the connection had been the fault of the Bristol train and 'they're Regional Railways, and we're South West Trains, you see'.

Mr Wilkins was not best pleased. The man at Bristol Temple Meads had been unequivocal: 'The ticket says Tisbury and I can guarantee that you will be got home one way or another,' he said. 'He had not been clear how this would be accomplished, but said that the most likely eventuality was that a taxi would be provided for me.' Mr Wilkins duly explained this to the manager at Salisbury who finally agreed to ring Bristol where, according to Mr Wilkins, 'fortunately, someone agreed to reimburse Salisbury station for my taxi fare and that of another passenger who had missed the last connection to Basingstoke'.

While waiting at Bristol, Mr Wilkins discovered another interesting facet of commercialisation. Alongside the passengers waiting for the train to Salisbury to arrive, there was a woman with a fully-laden buffet who was going on the same train to provide food and refreshments. The much-delayed and frazzled Mr Wilkins, desperate for a cup of tea, asked to buy one but the woman said she was not allowed to sell food or drinks on the platform. She explained that she had previously been 'told off' for doing so because the company for whom she worked only had a contract to sell its wares on the train. Mr Wilkins managed to persuade her to agree to sell him a cuppa if she were allowed to do so by the duty manager. Mr Wilkins duly approached the manager but, after a delay while the manager made a phone call, 'he came out on the platform to inform me that he did not "have the power" to give the buffet lady permission to sell refreshments to the delayed passengers. This was because she worked for the company to which catering had been subcontracted and was therefore not under his control. He did, however, helpfully arrange for a tannoy announcement to the effect that there was still a station buffet open across the bridge on platform 3.'

Mr Wilkins comments: 'These experiences that I had during the journey seem to exemplify the madness current in the railway system.'

Response: We wrote to the two train operating companies concerned, but neither replied.

Comment: The lesson in this is to get any promise in writing if it involves one train company delivering a service on behalf of another.

Railtrack's latest advice to intending passengers.

True stories from the Great Railway Disaster

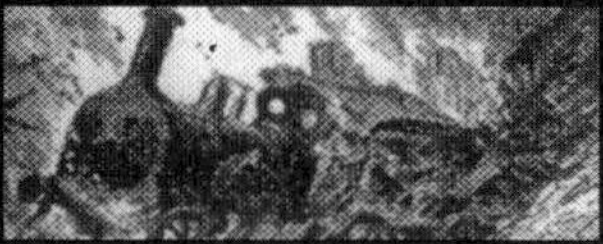

41. So You Want to Go the Long Way?

Fay Priestley of Selly Oak, Birmingham, was sent on a magical mystery tour of the Midlands thanks to the vagaries of information given out by different train operators. She has a Centro pass which allows her free travel in the West Midlands area. These type of passes are funded by local transport executives in several of the large conurbations around the country and therefore are valid only on certain British Rail trains. Ms Priestley recently made a weekend return journey from London to Birmingham. She bought a return ticket to Coventry, as her Centro pass allowed her free travel for the rest of the journey to Birmingham.

However, on the return journey from Birmingham, things began to get complicated. There was engineering work on the line between Birmingham and Coventry and the only through trains to London were routed via Nuneaton. Ms Priestley was told that as her Centro pass was not valid for trains to Nuneaton, she would have to take the bus provided by BR to Coventry and get a Euston train from there. She knew the bus took twice as long and was a less pleasant ride, but she did not want to pay any extra.

Imagine her surprise, then, when at Coventry, she found from the departure board that there were no trains to London. She continues the tale: 'Starting to panic, I finally located a cluster of railway staff back at the coach and asked for help: "There's a train for Nuneaton standing at platform 1," they said. "Hop on that" '. A cross-country journey brought her to Nuneaton where a station announcer said: 'Customers for London Euston, please cross to platform 4, where your train is waiting for you.' She says: 'I lugged my bags over the bridge and, yes, you've guessed it, this was the train from Birmingham New Street which my ticket had not allowed me to travel by.' She sighs: 'Not only could I have boarded it at Birmingham, I could have caught the one which left an hour earlier.'

Response: We wrote twice to Centro for its comments, but received no reply.

Comment: While these types of restrictions on tickets predate privatisation, they are part of the increasing disintegration of the formerly unified railway system and are bound to occur more frequently as competing companies take over, especially in situations such as these when emergency procedures are in operation.

Passengers for Birmingham get improved information for their next connection.

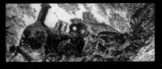
42. So You Want To Go The Other Way?

There are two railway routes between London and Southend: the London, Tilbury & Southend line from Fenchurch Street to Southend Central, and the Great Eastern from Liverpool Street to Southend Victoria. Regular commuters on the route used to be able to travel on either train interchangeably for an extra fee. Because the service on the Great Eastern is more reliable and has more modern trains than LTS, commuters on that line pay £168 more per year for a season ticket. So, in the old days, holders of Great Eastern season tickets costing £2,180 in 1995 were able to use either line completely interchangeably without any extra charge, while LTS season ticket holders had to pay a small supplement each time they wanted to use the other line, or alternatively, paid the £168 supplement to get an annual season ticket valid on both lines.

Now such inter-available tickets have been scrapped. Richard Delahoy, the chairman of the Southend Rail Travellers' Association, says they were particularly useful to people who spent the evening in London and returned on a late train because after 22.00 both services run from Liverpool Street. Now, if they get on the wrong train, they are charged the full fare: £9.20. This is because the two London to Southend lines are now considered alternative routes — as they are separate lines going to different termini at both ends — rather than through routes.

While tickets for through routes can be used for any journey between two stations, tickets for alternative routes are not interchangeable. Geddit?

Mr Delahoy said that there were all kinds of good reasons why the interchangeable tickets were useful: 'People might have a business meeting near Liverpool Street and find it easier to go back from there rather than get to Fenchurch Street. Or they might want to go to an intermediate station on the alternative line. They are, after all, paying over £2,000 for their annual ticket and this should entitle them to make maximum use of the railway.'

Response: The Southend Rail Travellers' Association has been involved in a long battle to get this situation changed, to no avail. Mr Delahoy wrote to the Rail Regulator, John Swift, pointing out that under the Railways Act 1993, the legislation which enables privatisation, the Regulator has a duty to protect the interests of rail passengers and to promote measures to encourage through journeys.

After a review of the policy which took a couple of months, Mr Swift wrote back to the Association saying that he was not going to intervene. He did concede that BR had wrongly failed to give proper notice of the change, but he argued that not enough complaints had been received to justify any action. Most importantly, Mr Swift stressed that he has a duty to promote competition and to promote efficiency and economy on the part of the railway operators as well as protecting users of the railway and said that he has to balance these duties. He concluded: 'I believe that the balance of advantage in this case lies in allowing the change to be made, not least because it will allow the operators greater freedom to introduce new products for the benefits of their passengers.' He added that the LTS board had reviewed the commercial case for the reintroduction of inter-available tickets but had decided against it.

A spokesman for LTS told the 'Mad' column: 'We view the lines as two adjacent ones, rather than a connected line. They are seen as separate railways, although LTS does run some late night trains from Liverpool Street.'

Comment: London to Southend is one of the few journeys on which there are two surviving alternative routes dating back to the 19th-century days of railway competition. It seems we are going to see something of a revival of that form of rivalry. According to Mr Delahoy: 'It seems people working for the two companies are settling old scores and doing everything they can to do each other down.' He says that

when Great Eastern ran a campaign to boost sales of their cheap day returns, they made sure there were enormous posters outside Southend Central and other LTS stations. And when LTS sponsored a flower bed for the local council, 'it happened to be outside Southend Victoria which I'm sure wasn't a coincidence'.

This issue goes to the heart of the conflicting duties of the regulator to promote both competition and to protect the rail passengers. These two duties do, at times, seem impossible to reconcile and Mr Swift is bound to be involved in a series of similar complaints. His reply does seem to suggest that if you have a complaint, make sure lots of other people write in as well, because clearly the volume of letters can affect decisions. It would be interesting to know whether, if more people had written, Mr Swift would have felt duty bound to reverse the situation.

43. So That's Why the Trains are Going Bumpety Bump in the Night?

People living next to the rail line in Bexhill-on-Sea have been wondering why they are being woken up by 'ghost trains' clattering at high speed through the town during the wee small hours on a previously sleepy line that runs along the Sussex coast between Hastings and Eastbourne.

The answer, local resident Richard Madge has discovered, lies in rail privatisation. Until 1994 Hastings had two train depots, St Leonards and Ore, which together serviced all rolling stock for local trains. Now the depot at Ore has been closed down and lies unused.

Under the break-up of the network introduced for privatisation, train services in the area are now run by two companies. The South Eastern train operating company runs the main service from Hastings to London via Tunbridge Wells, while the alternative route, via Bexhill, Eastbourne and Gatwick Airport is now run by Network SouthCentral.

Under the new system, the depot at St Leonards is now leased exclusively to SouthEastern, while the nearest Network SouthCentral depot is at Eastbourne. The trains needed to run the Network SouthCentral service therefore have to run empty along the 19 miles of track between the two towns at the beginning and end of each working day, providing a free and unwanted alarm service for the Bexhill residents.

Left: One bump in the night too many?

Right: Frustrated by the nature of railway privatisation, a diesel engine makes a dramatic bid for freedom.

44. So They Want to Tax Toy Trains?

Ever since the days of Hornby tinplate trains of the 1930s, rail companies have allowed model-railway makers free use of their logos. No longer. Toy trains are not immune from the widespread ramifications of rail privatisation.

Hornby, the country's largest train-set manufacturer has had to pay a fee of a few hundred pounds to two of the soon to be privatised railfreight companies for using logos on train sets. Grafar, another toy train manufacturer, based in Poole, Dorset, also reports that it is being charged for use of the logos and in a letter to a rail enthusiast, Chris Wright, the Managing Director Peter Graham Farish, managing director of Grafar, the Poole-based model train manufacturer, says that charging such amounts will result in the loss of 'an extremely attractive and cost free (to them) promotional opportunity for their companies'.

It is the freight companies hived off from BR that have been imposing these charges. Mainline freight, for example, has been making what it calls a small one-off charge for 'administrative costs' to toy makers. A spokeswoman said that this was because of the expense in providing information and artwork. Transrail freight also charges, but the innocence of a former age happily still lives on in the third of the freight companies. Richard Holmes of Loadhaul said: 'We would never dream of charging. We think it's a real compliment that the model manufacturers want to use our logo. It gives us excellent free publicity.'

Update/Comment: The three freight companies taken out of BR with all the fanfare of new liveries and logos are, in fact, being reunited under one banner. Together with Res, which also created for itself a completely new red livery, they have all been bought by Wisconsin Central, a US railfreight company. The exercise of having created three supposedly competing companies in 1994, only to merge them again early in 1996, less than two years after their break up, has been one of the most blatantly wasteful episodes of the rail privatisation process. As was pointed out many times by observers, railfreight, with just 6% of the market, faces enough competition from road without having to battle it out on rail. Most freight users welcome the arrival of an experienced private US company to bring new thinking into the sector, but many question the precise nature of the deal which allowed Wisconsin to take over both Res and the three freight companies. Whatever the ramifications of the sale, Wisconsin is unlikely to be so petty as to charge toy companies for the use of their logos.

Peter Graham Farish tells us that the situation has improved with most freight train companies seeing sense. He says that Railfreight Distribution, the company handling cross-Channel traffic, originally asked his firm for £7,000 for using their logos, and gradually reduced that to £750 and eventually they seemed to have accepted a lower amount just to cover the costs of the material needed to make accurate reproductions. He was still a bit bewildered by the whole episode: 'Some of the oil companies, like BP, help us enormously to make models because they know its good publicity for them.' Indeed, the model makers should actually charge the railways for giving them free advertising...

A member of Mainline's team of Trademark Protection Officers examines model trains for unauthorised use of the company's logo. A spokesman commented: 'We can make more from licensing model railway makers for the use of our logo than we can ever make from running trains.'

45. So it is the Wrong Type of Snowplough?

Next time Britain gets a blanket of snow, there may well be a new excuse for the ensuing disruption — there's no locomotive to push the snowplough.

Until the creation of Railtrack in April 1994, locomotives and snowploughs were all owned by British Rail. Now the locomotives have been taken over by the three freight companies which are being prepared for privatisation, while the snowploughs lie in separate yards run by Railtrack which is responsible for all track and infrastructure.

Railtrack does own a few locomotives for maintenance purposes, but these engines are not strong enough to push the ploughs. Stephen Joseph of the pressure group Transport 2000, who recently discovered this anomaly, says: 'This would never happen on the roads; the people responsible for clearing the roads own the snowploughs and just get on with it.' He says that the locomotives might well be in a completely different place from the ploughs, causing delays in getting the equipment out. Mr Joseph concludes: 'It just shows what is going on in the wacky world of privatisation.'

The matter was taken up by Jim Cousins, MP for Newcastle Central who says: 'This is just complete pottiness. We have had the wrong kind of snow — now we have got the wrong kind of snowplough. It is full of possibilities for people arguing with each other instead of tackling the job of serving the public.'

Response: Railtrack replied with such a heated response that clearly it is unlikely to snow near its headquarters ever again. Our old friend, Kate Smyth (see for example No 37), tells us rather

more about snowploughs than we ever asked: 'Railtrack has recently completed a wide-ranging condition survey of the snow-plough fleet, not only looking at the engineering condition of the ploughs, but where they are located. The fleet is now located in key depots around the country. There are three kinds of snowplough — miniature snow ploughs (up to 18in of snow for fitting to trains, patrol ploughs (snow up to 1.5m) and drift ploughs (snow over 1.5m deep). The ploughs are kept at depots around the country. We also have two snowblowers, one in Scotland, one in London.

'The snowploughs are used in conjunction with other proactive measures: point heaters, measures for wind-speed, snowmen, etc. Potential hazards are considered and when warnings are received from the Met Office... Railtrack zones implement a two-tier level of action (Frost Stage 1 & 2 and Snow Level 1 & 2).

'For evidence that Railtrack's policy works, we have only to point to the way that severe weather was dealt with this winter (1995/6). *Rail* magazine (Jan 17–30 1996) wrote: "Since April 1994, Railtrack has been updating winter precautions procedures and it is fair to say that the new regime has worked well, with good co-operation between the many and varied businesses and staff involved. Instructions were updated in December to further improve the system... Railtrack is on the job." '

Update: See previous item, No 44, for update on situation with the three freight companies.

Comment: It's nice to know that 'snowmen' are being used to clear away the snow. In the spirit of Raymond Briggs, we asked Railtrack for further details of how these snowmen perform the task. Do they build themselves out of the snow on the side of the track, or roll over picking up the snow? Unfortunately, Railtrack was unable to provide any further details.

We note that Ms Smyth does not deny that this equipment is now kept in separate locations. There was indeed chaos on the rails during the harsh winter of 1995/6 but since this was the worst weather in Britain for a generation, in the interest of fairness, it may be unwise to blame this policy for the delays and cancellations that inevitably resulted.

The author of the aforementioned Rail article, Murray Brown, did not quite write that Railtrack is on the job. In fact, he wrote: 'Whilst *Railtrack may be on the job*, the train operator must also play ball. When over 200 passengers were dumped at a deserted Swanley station in below zero temperatures off the 21.10 Victoria–Maidstone train on 6 December, there were no staff on duty and only one taxi driver who, fortunately, called for reinforcements!'

Incidentally, Mr Brown also points out that no one at BR actually ever used the famous 'wrong type of snow' expression: 'What happened was that BR's operations director was speaking to one of the London papers and mentioned *a type of snow* had caused problems. This was duly distorted to become a famous cliché and has gone down in folklore.'

'Hello. Is that Railtrack? I was wondering whether I could make a provisional booking for a snow plough for a week next Thursday?'

46. So You Want Your Connecting Train to Wait?

Roger Iredale travels daily from Whaley Bridge to Manchester's Oxford Road station every morning, but the train he catches terminates at Manchester Piccadilly, just before Oxford Road. Passengers who want to travel beyond Piccadilly can change trains at Stockport by simply crossing the platform and stepping into a waiting train that continues beyond Piccadilly. If they are both on time, the two trains coincide so that passengers can transfer between the two in a matter of seconds. Traditionally, if the arriving train has been slightly delayed, station staff have waited for a minute or so while passengers run across the short distance between the two.

No longer. Recently, Dr Iredale has noticed that the through train to Oxford Road has not waited, and he was particularly angered recently when the doors closed in his face as he ran across the platform followed by the closing of the doors of the train he had just left before he could get back into it. The platform staff entertained themselves by watching this fiasco, but did nothing to prevent it.

On making enquiries, Dr Iredale discovered that Railtrack fines the station operators if they delay any train even by one minute. A phone call is made from the Railtrack signalling staff to ask why the train was delayed and if the delay was caused by station staff, a fine is imposed which is totted up on a monthly or quarterly basis.

In other words, as Dr Iredale comments, 'Far from being responsive to passengers, the railway operators are now only interested in getting trains out of stations, regardless of whether they actually have passengers on them or not.'

Several other readers have written complaining about connecting trains no longer being held. John Heath of Chester was standing on platform 7 at Chester where the 17.49 Merseyrail train for Liverpool was waiting to leave. He describes the scene: 'On the other side of the same platform, a Regional Railways train bound for Manchester arrived from North Wales at precisely 17.49. At the very instant that it came to rest, the guard on the Merseyrail train blew the whistle, the automatic doors closed and it set off for Liverpool. Passengers from North Wales trying to make the connection frantically ran across the platform and chased the train, to no avail.'

When the platform manager was asked why the train for Liverpool had been released with passengers obviously trying to board it, he replied: 'That's Merseyrail, it's nothing to do with Regional Railways.'

Martin Taylor of Guildford points out that this failure to hold trains is not entirely new, as BR sometimes failed, but suggests that the new rivalry between different train operating companies has led to trains being deliberately timed to miss each other. He cites the example of Redhill where most trains are operated by Network SouthCentral, while the westward line to Guildford and Reading is run by Thames Trains. He writes: 'Thames is mainly interested in carrying passengers from Gatwick Airport and does not want its westbound services to be delayed at Redhill. Therefore, many trains seem to be deliberately timed to leave one minute before the arrival of a Network SouthCentral service in order to avoid making a connection. In addition, platform staff have been told not to hold Thames services to wait for late-running Network SouthCentral trains. The argument that greater inconvenience will be caused to passengers already on the train is not valid because a few minutes delay' can easily be made up before the Thames service reaches Reading.'

Update/Comment: John Watts, the railways minister, later allayed all fears about connecting trains when in the autumn of 1995, in a TV interview, he promised that with privatisation all the trains would run on time and therefore there would be no need for connecting trains to be held while waiting for delayed services.

In January 1996, Railtrack announced its performance regime which monitors some 13,000 points around the network. Unlike the Passenger's Charter, the monitoring includes taking observations at intermediate points during a train's journey, and not just at the terminus. Any delay beyond 3min — not one as stated by Dr Iredale's informant — is then investigated to find out who caused it and a penalty imposed on the culprit. The average cost of a minute's delay is around £30, according to Railtrack, which makes the taxi fares a better option very quickly — though, of course, environmentally it is wasteful and, moreover, the money then goes out of the rail system to the taxi operators, rather than, as under the old system, staying in it if the train is delayed slightly, creating only internal costs for the railway. While better monitoring and the creation of a performance regime are undoubted improvements, the fact that money, rather than the needs of passengers, is at the centre of the system will inevitably lead to doors being slammed in the face of passengers trying to catch trains, and a greatly increased use of taxis for passengers who have missed the last train of the day. (See No 57 below re further use of taxis.)

47. So You Want a Clean Track?

Travellers to and from Brighton have been appalled at how dirty the track outside the station has been getting, likening it to a rubbish dump. As the local paper, the *Brighton and Hove Leader* put it on 16 November 1995: 'Excrement and litter on the tracks at Brighton station have been allowed to mount up for the last eight months.'

The reason for the build-up of rubbish is that no one has been given responsibility for cleaning up the track as the contract has not been awarded. David Lepper, chairman of Brighton Council's economic development committee, says there is a potential health hazard from rats, and the litter could also cause braking problems for the trains. He told the local paper: 'Before, if something needed to be done at Brighton, it would be handled by local staff. Now there is no overall control.' Staff at the station report hundreds of complaints and Chris Randall, public relations manager of Network SouthCentral, the main user of the station, said: 'We have no power to intervene,' as the matter is the responsibility of Railtrack.

Railtrack claims it has had no complaints and a spokesman told the *Leader* that cleaning 'used to be quite easy to organise, but since the break-up of the railway services, it's not. Now every task has to have a job order number.' He added that negotiations to award a contract are still going on: 'It takes a long time to award a contract. People working on the track need to be safety trained and you can't do that overnight.'

There were similar complaints along the coast at Chichester where local resident Bill Mason reports that 'Chichester residents have been forced to watch their once neat and tidy station deteriorate into a rubbish tip. The tracks are overflowing with rubbish and have not been cleared for months.'

While staff at Chichester told Mr Mason that they would like to clean the track, they are not allowed to do so because they work for the local train operator and the track is the responsibility of Railtrack. Mr Mason, who feared that the rubbish was a potential fire hazard, was told that if the litter did catch fire, the station staff would not be allowed to use an extinguisher to put it out. When he complained, in August 1995, to BR, he was told that Railtrack, who took over responsibility for the track in April 1994, had not yet finalised a contract for the work. The local *Chichester Observer* on 31 August 1995 was told by BR that 'contracts were at a fairly embryonic stage and some points needed to be ironed out'. Chichester Society chairman Reg Davis-Poynter is reported as commenting: 'Chichester railway station used to be a showpiece. Now it's a disgrace.' Chichester firefighters had, it was reported, attended three fires on the line near the city.

Response: Peter Dring, public affairs manager, Railtrack south zone, responded to our letter with a sad tale. He wrote: 'Briefly, after we took over responsibility for track clearance in April 1995, we removed rubbish from between the platforms at Brighton station on three occasions, in May, August and November.

'In organising the work, we were faced with two major difficulties. Under health and safety regulations, the job now can only be done by properly trained staff. To comply with that, we have been using our existing maintenance contractors, but they have also been busy dealing with other routine work, some of which has safety implications and has to be given a higher priority than track litter clearance. Also, because the electric current has to be switched off before rubbish can be removed, we try to do it at night to avoid service disruptions. But that is exactly when our contractor is busiest anyway.'

Mr Dring concludes: 'We are committed to keeping tracks in stations as clear as we can, but we don't have unlimited resources and have to use them as effectively as possible for the railway as a whole. A dedicated litter clearance contract has been drawn up and when it is let we hope the situation will rapidly improve.'

His letter was much more diplomatic than the response to *Private Eye* which, in its final issue of 1995, quoted a Railtrack spokesman as saying: 'We don't put the litter there. It's litter the public discard. Obviously it's not nice for the travelling public — who are not our customers but they do travel on our infrastructure.'

Update: After pressure from the Association of Metropolitan Authorities and passenger groups, the Government was forced to bring in legislation in the spring of 1996 to ensure that Railtrack had a legal responsibility to clean the track. Ministers admitted that there had been a loophole created when the act to privatise the railways was passed in 1993. For its part, Railtrack said that it had taken on the task of cleaning its 23,000 miles of track voluntarily but clearly from the incidents outlined above, this commitment had not always been carried out properly.

Comment: So, why has Railtrack employed a contractor who is already busy at night to do the work? Somebody was clearly doing this work before April 1995 and surely Railtrack could have employed them to do the work.

There is one valid point arising from this. The safety regime on the railways has become incredibly onerous, creating a whole bureaucracy before anyone can go along the line. While no one would question the need for a high standard of safety, figures from the Railways Inspectorate suggest that these procedures have not led to a reduction in accidents to staff and contractors on the railway, and have merely led to additional costs. The extra costs make the railways overall more expensive and therefore less attractive to passengers who may, instead, put their lives at risk by driving their car, a form of travel several hundred times more dangerous than rail. Therefore an over-obsessive attitude towards rail safety can be detrimental to society at large and lead to more road accidents. This type of consideration will be even more difficult to take into account when the rail network is privatised than under a nationalised structure.

Mindless vandals add to Railtrack's problems; not only is litter dropped but the running rails are stolen as well.

48. So You Want to Take a Taxi from the Station?

Passengers arriving at Cambridge station have been surprised that taxis no longer wait at the rank next to the station but on the approach road a couple of hundred yards away. Passengers have had to lug their bags and push their trolleys to the new taxi parking place. Anne-Marie Ellis had to wait on the blustery pavement for 10min on a freezing day in December and asked the taxi driver why they no longer used the rank. He said the charges had been increased dramatically by the company running the station and the taxi drivers were therefore boycotting the rank.

West Anglia Great Northern, which rents the station from Railtrack, confirms that the taxi drivers are no longer using the rank. Previously, taxi owners belonging to the local association paid £117 a year for the use of the rank, but in a recent review WAGN increased this to £324. After negotiations, the company knocked this down to £290 but the drivers still refuse to pay.

Response: A spokesman for WAGN explained that the increase had arisen out of an attempt to equalise the charges between two sets of taxi drivers, those belonging to the licensed drivers association and those who were not members of the association. In the past, the 120 drivers who belonged to the association were only required to pay the lower charge of £117, while the non-members were charged several hundred pounds. The change had been an attempt to ensure that all drivers paid the same

amount. He added that 'charges in Cambridge were lower than in other comparable cities'.

Update: This item aroused considerable national interest and was broadcast on both Radio 4 and Radio 2. The railways minister, John Watts, gave the following response to the *You and Yours* programme: 'This is not something which arises out of privatisation at all. The root of this is a dispute between two different groups of taxi operators, the licensed taxi operators association in Cambridge and the non-licensed. In the past, the licensed taxi drivers association had a very big concession in relation to others and the train operator last year decided to level the playing field between the two types of operator.' In response to the interviewer's question that the root cause was the requirement to raise rents for Railtrack, he said: 'There's been no significant increase in the cost of rent at the station.'

This misses the point, since before the break-up of the railway into its 100 or so component parts, this exchange of rents between the various companies within the railway simply did not take place. The basic point is that the railway should be about providing a rail service, and not about raising rents from taxi drivers, who are providing part of the overall transport service, to subsidise it.

Members of Railtrack's staff at Cambridge unload the new self-propelled taxi units for passengers' use at the station.

49. So You Want to Charter a Train?

One of the hidden casualties of rail privatisation has been the charter train. Many organisations which used to charter trains for trips to London or seaside towns have found the price has increased exponentially, deterring them from arranging the journey.

One such is the 7,000-strong Bournemouth Rail Travel Association which, until recently, used to charter trains to London and charge its members around £12 return. No longer. When the association tried to charter a train recently, it was told by South West Trains that the fee for a 472-seater train had more than doubled to £9,500, which works out at over £20 per seat before any administrative charges can be added on. So the association cancelled its proposed trip with its spokesman saying the new situation 'was the economics of the madhouse'. He reckons that it results 'directly from the fragmentation of the railway industry into a multitude of accounting units as a prelude to privatisation. The railway industry is shifting away from the concept of public service. It will become a cosy cartel of private monopolies.'

George Willey of the *Swanage Advertiser* who questioned South West Trains about this increase was told by the company that it cannot make an accurate estimate of the cost of providing a train because 'there are six departments involved, each setting its own charges and each having to make a profit'. The Department of Transport's explanation is that charter trains were, in the past, subsidised and this is why prices have gone up as this financial support has been removed.

Mr Willey, however, sees it differently: 'The new motto of the railways must be "Don't let the train take the strain." '

Update: It would be possible to fill this whole book with tales about the *débâcle* over rail charters (see, for example, No 27). There has been a dramatic reduction in the number of charter trains as a result of experiences like that of the Bournemouth group. After the reorganisation of the railways in April 1994 when Railtrack was created, the responsibility for hiring out locomotives and crew was given to Rail Express Systems, which runs the mail trains.

With Res charging exorbitant amounts for the crew and traction, and Railtrack levying high access fees, the charter business became uneconomic. Under the old BR regime, the charters were only expected to cover their marginal costs, the extra expenditure they caused the railways. They were not expected to give BR a profit, or contribute to the overall costs of running the railway which was there as a public service to be used as much as possible.

As Nigel Harris pointed out in a detailed article in *Rail* magazine in October 1995, excursions were not just valuable in themselves, giving people a good day's outing in an environmentally sound way, but they had the added benefit of encouraging people to try out the railways. Some of these people might indeed decide to use rail again. Mr Harris wrote: 'Part of the answer is that, sadly, a great deal of the common sense which characterised the railway seems to have died with the marginal economics which made excursions possible. Excursions are now run by third parties who have to buy access to the main lines, with their traction and staff, from a railway whose only remit is to ensure that each train carries its costs and makes a profit. Nobody looks at the bigger picture; wider benefits are no longer relevant in the tunnel vision of today's managers.'

The biggest charter company was owned by Pete Waterman, who made a fortune out of pop music. Waterman Railways became the first organisation to take over part of the old BR when it bought the special trains business, which ran many of the charter trains, in April 1994. It owns eight locomotives and 270 coaches but decided to pull out of the charter business in the late summer of 1995 because the company felt it was impossible to run them economically, and restricted itself to hiring out its equipment.

Comment: If anything shows that the economics of the rail industry under the privatised regime do not make sense it is the story of the Bournemouth charter and countless others like it. The fact that it is not viable to run a charter from Bournemouth to London and back, even with every seat filled, demonstrates that the new railway financing regime has completely distorted transport economics. The Government's argument is that these high charges reflect the real cost if the original spending on investment is taken into account. That is shown to be ridiculous by contrasting the costs of rail charter with those of the air industry. Just note, for example, the fact that planes can be chartered for as little as, say, £80 per seat for a return journey to Spain, taking into account all the costs, since this is virtually an entirely private sector business.

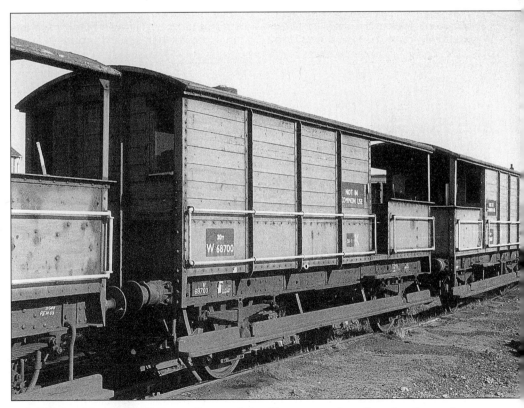

InterCity Great Western launches its new charter train set.

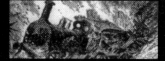

50. So You Want to Open a New Station?

Years of trying to get a station at Ashchurch in Gloucestershire reopened have been put at risk by rail privatisation. Chris Shaw, the borough planning officer for Tewkesbury is appalled by the escalating cost of the project, much of it caused by the reorganisation of the railways in preparation for privatisation.

In 1992, reopening was estimated to cost £353,000 and a similar project at Cam/Dursley on the Gloucester to Bristol line was costed at £433,000. Mr Shaw says that because Cam/Dursley was more likely to attract people away from their cars and on to

rail, it was the first priority and opened in May 1994 at a cost of £560,000. By that time, however, the cost of the Ashchurch project had risen to £530,000 and by February 1995 it was £600,000. Then, the real horror. Mr Shaw writes: 'By June 1995, the estimated cost, as advised by Railtrack, had risen to an astonishing £1,025,000. Councillors are incredulous that in a little over a year, the cost of the project has escalated by 193 per cent.'

Mr Shaw reckons that the implications of this type of increase are that 'no further station reopenings will

take place in the county while project costs remain at this inflated level'. He points out that this is contrary to the type of planning policies to get people out of their cars which are being promoted by the government. He comments: 'Judiciously sited, new stations can make substantial contributions to reducing reliance on the private car and thereby the reduction in carbon dioxide emissions.' On rail privatisation he says: 'It is understood that this phenomenon is not limited to Gloucestershire but has been experienced throughout the country. It is clear that in this case a heavy price is being paid by the community to the obvious benefit of no one but future rail company shareholders.'

Response/Comment: At a meeting between railway management and councillors, Railtrack explained the cost increase by saying that the parts of British Rail supplying engineering services are being prepared for privatisation and have been 'learning about the costs involved in sub-contracting'. This has apparently led to significant increases in their estimates for the station works. Mr Shaw cites some examples: 'Because the site workers are no longer British Rail employees, safety supervision now has to be purchased at a cost of £70,000 in this case.' He says a further example of increased cost is that Railtrack has penalty clauses in its train path contracts with the train operating companies such that if engineering works result in the delay of a train, then compensation is payable. This estimated cost, which of course may never actually result, has been added to the station costing. (Presumably, the train operating company will then be charged extra both for having another station at which its trains stop and for renting the station.) Mr Shaw retorts: 'It can therefore be demonstrated that at least a substantial part of this virtual doubling of project cost is directly due to privatisation arrangements.'

It does seem that there is an element of Railtrack trying it on. But then it is a monopoly supplier of rail services, deliberately created as such by the Government. It is like British Gas, which demands advance payment for services such as moving meters which only British Gas is able to carry out. (See also No 38 above.)

Update: Negotiations were still continuing as this book went to press.

This week's good cause: due to the ever-increasing costs involved with constructing new stations work has had to stop at this site. Please give generously!

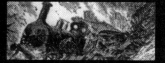

51. So You Want the Train to Stop at Your Local Station?

Residents of King's Langley in Hertfordshire were annoyed when North London Railways reduced the number of trains stopping at their station during the late evening from two to one an hour. Local parish councillors met the rail company to seek an explanation. Councillor Paul Tucker reported from the meeting: 'They refused to reinstate the service on two grounds: first, that customers travelling to Milton Keynes would resent the 6min delay to their journey, and fundamentally because they would have to pay Railtrack more money to stop the train at the station than just run through it.'

The councillors asked for more information such as details of the company's customer research on which it based its assumptions about the views of the Milton Keynes passengers, and details of how much extra stops at the station would cost North London Railways. They were told this information could not be given to them because it was 'commercial in confidence' and might prejudice a potential bidder for the line.

John Prime, a commuter from King's Langley, said that he and hundreds of others travel regularly through the station and none have heard any complaints from Milton Keynes passengers about the delay caused by stopping at King's Langley. 'The reasons given by North London Railways are bizarre.'

He adds: 'The logic of this argument, together with Railtrack's method of charging, seems to be that no train should ever stop until it reaches its final destination.' Perhaps Mr Prime should keep this to himself, in case someone in the rail industry thinks it is a good idea.

Response: Graham Bashford, Corporate Affairs Manager of North London Railways, wrote: 'The number of services provided at any particular station is driven largely by demand. Prior to the two late night trains ceasing to stop at King's Langley a survey showed that a total of 18 people alighted at the station from trains departing Euston between 22.00 and 23.34. A survey carried out at other smaller stations revealed a similar situation. At the larger stations 50 or more people were alighting from each train. By not stopping at smaller stations used by very few people, long distance journey times are reduced, moreover customers' perception over 'fast' and 'slow' trains has to be taken into account.

'There would seem to be some misunderstanding in the article as to the reasons for the withdrawal of the stop at King's Langley which was implemented for the benefit of the vast majority of users of the service. I hope the situation is now clarified. The last two sentences in the article are, of course, complete nonsense.'

Update: Geoff Hemingway of Leigh-on-Sea suggested a mischievous solution to this problem. He wrote: 'The solution to the problem might be for the good commuters wishing to alight at King's Langley simply to arrange to take it in turns to pull the communication cord at the appropriate moment? I believe the standard operating procedure when this occurs is that the train stops at the next station; perhaps, after a few such emergency halts, North London Railways would get the message?' We, at the 'Mad' railway column could not, of course, possibly recommend such irresponsible behaviour.

Comment: This habit of Railtrack charging extra for trains which stop (see also No 27) is one of the great absurdities of the new structure of the railways. There is clearly no extra cost in terms of track wear and tear, or signalling staff (who would have to be there anyway) of a train stopping or just going through a station. (Does Railtrack reimburse train operating companies when trains fail to stop at stations because the line is too slippery, as happens sometimes in the autumn?) It is clearly just a way for Railtrack to assess and charge revenue, but it in no way reflects a real cost. And far from encouraging train operators to be sensitive to passengers' needs, it is a financial incentive for them to reduce the number of station stops which, at the end of the day, are for the benefit of passengers.

52. So You Want to Travel as a Group With a Discount?

For many years, Susan and Tim O'Brien have organised the travel arrangements for the Aston Villa London supporters' group. Each summer, they used to be sent a contract to ensure that the supporters' club qualified for the discounts available for group travel. Now life is about to get more complicated.

Tony Natchingall, the retail and customer services manager London–West Midlands, (the job titles are so snappy in the new railway) has warned the O'Briens that there will now have to be a massive increase in the paperwork they have to complete.

A letter from Mr Natchingall told the O'Briens: 'British Rail has now been split into 25 different train operating companies. It will now be necessary to sign a separate contract for each route you travel on and each contract will need to be signed by two people. The address needs to be that of the first signature and the organisation they represent.' He added that unless the contracts were signed, 'no special rates would be available'.

Mr O'Brien is bewildered by the extra paperwork and has wondered about taking everybody on coaches instead.

The club is also being forced to change the train which it normally takes to Birmingham for home matches. The group used to travel on the 11.05 from Euston to allow a bit of time in the pub before the match started at 3pm. However, InterCity West Coast has taken a coach off the Saturday trains. The explanation given to Mr O'Brien was that under privatisation, each carriage resulted in extra charges being paid to Railtrack and therefore there was pressure to save money by shortening the trains.

Since the 11.05 goes on to Wolverhampton, the Wolves' London contingent also use that train and there is no longer room to take both supporters' groups. Therefore, the O'Briens and their merry band of claret and blue supporters have to take the earlier train which makes it difficult for their members outside London, from places such as Ramsgate and Brighton, to travel. Mr O'Brien notes, too, that an average of 15min has been added to the schedule of the train over the past few years, which he reckons makes it easier for the company to meet its Passenger's Charter figures.

Response: George Reynolds, the public affairs manager of InterCity West Coast replied to the item saying it 'missed the mark', although it seems to confirm the point Mr O'Brien makes about the extra bureaucracy. He wrote: 'InterCity West Coast has enjoyed an excellent relationship over the years with many football supporters who use the trains. At present these clubs have a contract with British Rail which qualifies them for special rates. In future that same contract will be with the individual train operating company on whose trains the fans will be travelling. It is unlikely any supporters will need contracts with each of the 25 operating companies.'

On the point about the coach, Mr Reynolds contradicts what Mr O'Brien was told previously by InterCity West Coast. Mr Reynolds writes: 'It is claimed the Aston Villa London supporters' group, normally between

12 and 16 people, are now unable to travel on their usual 11.05 Euston–Birmingham train "because a coach has been taken off Saturday trains". Not true. The formation of this service has not been altered although from time to time a coach may be taken out of a train for operational purposes.'

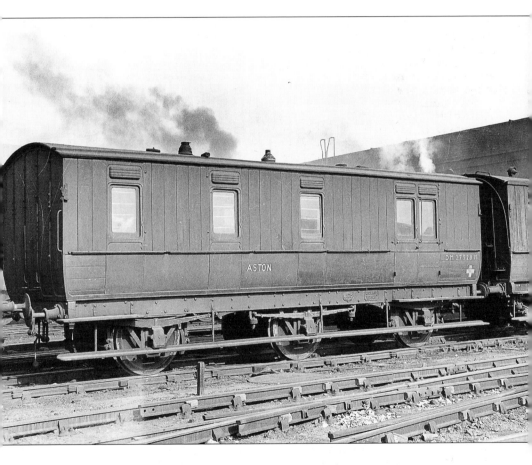

Privatisation has some benefits. It is now possible for individual football supporters' clubs to have their own sponsored coach; unfortunately our photographer recorded this vehicle before the transformation was completed.

53. So You Want to Get to or From Stockport?

Stockport seems to be the centre of chaos when it comes to lack of co-ordination between the rail companies, as Tim Gallagher and Dr Roger Iredale recently and separately both found out. Both were victims of an apparent unwillingness of the companies to co-operate in the event of a breakdown.

Dr Iredale found himself stranded at Stockport when a train in front of his broke down, blocking the two behind it. When he asked why his train could not be backed out and continue by way of another platform, he was told: 'The track is owned by Railtrack and we need to get permission at a high level before we can do anything like that.'

Mr Gallagher had a similar experience just after Christmas when the train he was taking from Euston to Stockport shuddered to a halt near Rugby. As a regular user of the infamous InterCity West Coast line, he was not surprised at the breakdown. But he was not expecting a 4hr wait for another engine and driver.

The conductor informed the restless passengers that although a spare engine was available at Rugby, it did not belong to InterCity West Coast and could not, therefore, be used. Instead, an engine was located in Wolverhampton; but because of the delay, another driver had to be found as the original one had worked his hours. A driver finally had to be summoned from London.

Mr Gallagher eventually reached Stockport at 00.45, over four hours late, and then found that the promised complimentary taxis had failed to materialise.

Response/Update:

George Reynolds of InterCity West Coast denied that passengers would ever be kept waiting for a locomotive. He wrote: 'The InterCity West Coast policy in the event of a locomotive failure, is to hire the nearest available appropriate locomotive to assist.'

However, Clare Short, Labour's transport spokeswoman, obtained a leaked memo in February 1996 which showed this is not the case throughout the railway. The memo, addressed to signalboxes from the area production manager of Railtrack North West, P. Tattersall, and dated 7 February 1996, says: 'As you may be aware, if Railtrack have to use locomotives to clear the Main Line due to a third party failure, we are normally charged £2,000 per time.

'Therefore, because of various contractual/penalty issues, it *may* (his italics) make more commercial sense to let the owner of the failed train arrange his own assistance.

'Therefore, all requirements for the hire of locos *must be* dealt with via the zonal control — only they have the authority to obtain assisting locomotives. The only exception to this is when a life-threatening/serious *safety* issue requires immediate action — eg a vehicle on fire — in such circumstances the decision should quickly be ratified with the Zonal Control.'

This letter clearly shows that commercial considerations are sometimes placed above the need to get stranded trains moving as quickly as possible and also that the bureaucratic procedures needed to be undertaken — checking with zonal control — appear to be an inevitable source of further delay to passengers stuck in broken down trains.

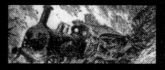

Beth Follini of Peckham, south London, was planning a weekend trip with friends to Fishguard, Wales, and looked up the train services in her timetable. Although it appeared that Great Western ran two trains a day, when she rang to check, she was told that no trains went to Fishguard on the day she wished to travel as it was a holiday, and she would have to go to a station 40 miles away.

After double-checking her timetable, Ms Follini could not believe that there were no trains, and phoned a different number. This time she was told that while there were no services to Fishguard, she could catch a train to Clarbeston Road, a mere 15 miles away.

She then went to Euston and bought Apex tickets for herself and one of her friends. But when the rest of the party went to book, they were told that there was a train that ran directly to Fishguard after all.

Rather annoyed, Ms Follini and her friend attempted to change their tickets in order to join the rest of their group on the more direct service. They were told they would be unable to switch, as the two lines were run by different companies and the Apex tickets would not be accepted by Great Western to Fishguard.

After complaining that they had purchased the Clarbeston Road tickets only because they had been misinformed, Ms Follini was told that the lack of co-ordination in regard to timetabling was a result of privatisation.

Not only was Ms Follini not allowed to switch the tickets, she was also refused a refund to cover the price of the taxi journey from Clarbeston Road to Fishguard.

She comments: 'Because of rail privatisation, we had to pay for a taxi from Fishguard to Clarbeston Road and we were deprived of travelling back as a merry group.'

In a desperate effort to improve passenger information Railtrack seek inspiration from alien railway operators.

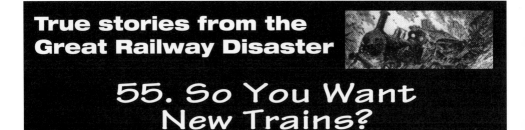

55. So You Want New Trains?

Passengers on services in West Yorkshire between Leeds, Bradford, Ilkley and Skipton are bemused by the fact that they have a newly refurbished electrified line operated with trains that only just missed out on World War 2.

The electrification was completed last autumn and was part of an effort to attract people out of their cars and back on to trains. West Yorkshire Passenger Transport Authority, which subsidises local services, approached various finance houses with the idea of arranging to lease new trains, a method the Government has been supporting.

The train manufacturers, desperately short of work, were delighted at the prospect of new orders and the cost would have been about £3 million per year. The finance companies, however, were worried about the long term prospects for the train services.

Mick Lyons, chairman of the PTA, explains: 'They asked us what would happen if, in a few years' time, the services were privatised and the new company wanted to use its own trains, not the new ones.' Because of their concern, the finance houses would advance money for the trains only if the PTA guaranteed that it would pay the whole price — £40 million — within seven days of a change of ownership being announced. 'We couldn't do that,' said Mr Lyons, 'so the deal fell through.'

In the meantime, to keep services running, the PTA found some 30- to 35-year-old Class 308 trains discarded by Network SouthEast which BR let it have free as long as they were refurbished. That cost about £4 million for the 20 sets of coaches. Now it seems they will have to remain on the line for years to come.

And what is most galling for the PTA and the rail passengers of West Yorkshire is that the old trundlers cost £3 million per year, not much less than the PTA would have paid for brand-new trains. That is because all coaches are now owned by the three highly profitable rolling stock companies, the Roscos, which were sold to the private sector late in 1995 for £1.8 billion. Between them they own all the trains on the rail network.

The Roscos charge very high rates for leasing out their stock and the Government has so far refused the PTA permission to lease new stock. Soon, the PTA, which is responsible for maintenance of the coaches, will be faced with having to pay for the second refurbishment of the old trains to keep them on the rails.

Mr Lyons comments: 'How can we attract people on to the railways if we can't provide them with new trains? The whole basis of the refurbishment scheme costing £80 million was that there would be new stock. Now we're paying the same amount to operate with old trains, which are not attracting as many people out of their cars as new trains would.'

Update: As of February 1996, nothing had changed. Mr Lyons was still trying to negotiate with the Government but had made no progress. Vanessa Bridge, the transport correspondent of the *Yorkshire Evening Post,* pointed out that the old 308 trains had a rather dangerous tendency: 'There is a history of the doors of these trains exploding. There was a case in Leeds station in November 1995 when a door was blown off the hinges a few minutes after the passengers had left the train.' She said that there had been similar cases when the trains were used by Network SouthEast and that it was caused by a problem with the central electric motors which occasionally self-ignited.

Nicholas Preston of Skipton pointed out a further twist. He explained that the old diesel trains weren't that bad: 'The real irony of this situation is that the diesel units which provided the service on these routes were only around 10 years old and quite acceptable, if perhaps not available in enough numbers.' He adds that in order to educate the 'passengers, sorry customers' in the ways of the old trains, Railtrack had to erect instruction posters on how to open the doors at the stations. Mr Preston said: 'The posters explained that you lower the window of the door from which you wish to exit, lean out and use the handle outside. Amazing, I wonder if it will catch on.'

Response: John Watts, the railways minister, said in Parliament in response to a question by Max Madden, one of the local MPs, that the purchase of rolling stock 'was up to the operator'.

Comment: This is not the only problem faced by PTAs. As shown by the Bolton toilets incident (see No 16), investments by the PTAs have been made very difficult under the new system. The West Yorkshire PTA spent many months negotiating with Railtrack over improvements to Leeds station. The difficulty was that if the refurbishment were carried out, it would result in increased rents payable to Railtrack, even though the PTA had already paid for the improvements itself. Although a successful solution to that conundrum seems to have been found, it took extensive negotiation, and similar problems have arisen around the country. Therefore, far from encouraging investment, the new system seems to make it more difficult.

As for Mr Watts, he appears to have ignored the fact that any purchase of rolling stock by the PTA would have to be sanctioned by the Government.

True stories from the Great Railway Disaster

56: So You Want the Cheapest Fare?

Railtrack's crack team of ticketing experts desperately seek a rational reason for the latest fares policy.

As the rail network is being split into 25 companies, the Government has had to introduce new national conditions of carriage, the rules and regulations governing the sale of tickets. Mark Holdstock of the BBC Radio 4 *You and Yours* programme discovered that the new rules create unforeseen problems for some rail passengers.

Mr Holdstock was planning to go on a round trip from Durham, down to London, back up to Edinburgh and then returning to Durham, a journey he had done many times. Under the old rules, he would book himself two SuperSavers covering both legs of the journey — Durham–London and back, and London–Edinburgh and back, at a cost of around £83. However, under the new regulations published in January 1996, he could only use these two tickets in combination on the return trip if the train actually stopped at Durham on the way back. However, from the timetable, the journey was not feasible, because if he left London on the 18.30 train which stops at Durham, he would miss the connection to Edinburgh. The alternative was to leave on the earlier Durham train, go to Newcastle, and wait an hour to pick up the Edinburgh train.

He comments: 'It seems all too complicated and an unnecessary inconvenience.' And, he says, if he wants to avoid all that hassle, all he has to do is buy three singles, which would cost £143, nearly twice the fare.

Comment: There are some advantages to the new conditions in that, for example, passengers are now *entitled* to compensation if they are delayed, whereas previously it had been discretionary. But we see the obsession of promoting competition entering into the equation with changes such as those to the SuperSaver tickets outlined above.

'When they said the cheapest fare was only £10.00, I thought that at least I'd get to sit on the train.'

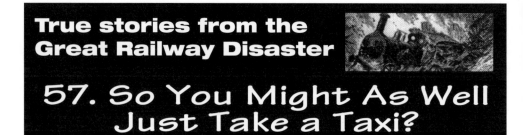
57. So You Might As Well Just Take a Taxi?

John Ringham went to meet his wife off a train at Windermere in the autumn of 1995. She was due to change at Oxenholme, near Kendal, and the train was due in at 22.15.

He explains: 'She telephoned me from the train to say that they were running half an hour late. In case they made up time, I arrived to pick her up at Windermere station well before the

train was due in. The car park, the waiting rooms, the booking office and the platform were in total darkness.'

At 22.15, the connecting train arrived but none of the passengers who disembarked were from the London train. Mr Ringham says: 'Three of us went to see the driver and asked him about the London passengers. He told us he knew nothing about that, that it was a different company and was not his business and took the train out again.'

Half an hour later, a fleet of taxis — seven or eight strong — arrived, one of which carried Mrs Ringham.

She told Mr Ringham that the Windermere passengers had been called together by a railway official at Oxenholme and told that they would complete their journey by taxi. The company operating the connecting train apparently charged InterCity West Coast, which ran the London train, £60 per minute to wait for the London connection and 'therefore it was much cheaper to take ongoing passengers by taxi'.

Update: Many similar stories have been submitted to the 'Mad' column. Indeed, the *Lakes Line* bulletin which covers the very branch line mentioned in this item, reports an identical incident at Oxenholme in March where the train was only 7min late, but nevertheless the Windermere train had left. Indeed, the author reports that the passengers then had to wait so long for their taxi that they actually saw the Windermere train coming into Oxenholme station on its way back '3min early'. The author points out that 'holding the connection for 10min would have saved the taxi fares (of £17.50 to Windermere) and at least 5min could have been saved with a quick turnround at Windermere, causing very little disruption to any other services.

Winifred Maguire of King's Lynn recounts a friend of hers missing a connection to King's Lynn, 'although her train from York was only a few minutes late at Peterborough. It was explained to her that trains travelling in certain directions no longer waited for connecting trains from other directions because they belonged to a different section of the system now.' She adds that BR was quite happy to provide her and four other passengers with free taxis at a cost of £64.

Nick Odgers arrived at Truro at 17.20 one evening only to be told that as the train was 8min late, the 17.15 to Falmouth had gone because 'they are not allowed to hold a train any more'. British Rail, he says, had to pay for a taxi, just for him, to get back to Penmere.

58. So That's Why It's Getting Cramped in the Signalbox

Barrie Clement, Labour editor of *The Independent*, reported in January 1996 on the chaos in a London signalbox resulting from the split up of the network. He wrote: 'As our railway system enters the cut and thrust of the market place, one signalbox seems to be taking on the atmosphere of a dealing room in the City of London. At Liverpool Street the brashness of the financial barrow boy has apparently invaded the tranquillity of what is now described as a control centre. Signal operators at their 'state of the art workstations' can hardly hear themselves think on occasion. The problem is that sitting cheek-by-jowl with the signal staff are representatives of the five train operating groups using Liverpool Street, according to exasperated union officials. They are Great Eastern Railway, Anglia Railways, West Anglia Great Northern, LTS rail and the Freight Trains Group.'

Mr Clement reports that each company wants to ensure that its trains should not be disadvantaged when the timetable is disrupted by 'leaves on the line, the wrong kind of snow and other unthinking acts of an unprivatised God'.

For example, the freight company representative will seek to ensure that his trains are not always shunted off into sidings to allow the InterCity expresses run by Anglia smooth passage. Similarly, 'the man from West Anglia Great Northern will be keen to see that the Flash Harrys of InterCity are not placated at the expense of his crowded commuter trains'.

There is, according to Mr Clement, one man presiding over this hubbub,

the equivalent of the Fat Controller in the *Thomas the Tank Engine* books. He is the chap from Railtrack, charged with adjudicating between the competing interests.

According to those familiar with the signalbox, the noise sometimes resembles 'an Arabian souk'. Mr Clement reports: 'It has got so bad that signal staff have threatened to shut the system down unless the people from the train operators restrain themselves. The language has been known to approach the colourful.'

Peter King, the Rail, Maritime and Transport workers' local official believes the clamour could undermine safety because the usual complement for the centre is around two dozen at most and now there are up to 34 people in the box. He says: 'Our people have to speak to drivers and other signalboxes on the phone. Sometimes they can't hear themselves think. They are often forced to whisper so that the train operators can't hear them and argue the toss over their decisions. It can get very stressful at times. Basically, it's insane.'

Railtrack put up screens to deaden the noise, but some had to be taken away because there was not enough room in the box, according to Mr King.

Mr Clement explains that the increase in personnel in the box is entirely down to the break-up of the railways. 'Before the break-up of BR, there was a staff of around a dozen, including a BR controller who made all the decisions about which services should take priority.'

The RMT is worried that identical problems could develop in larger control centres all over the network as companies insist on all having their 'four pennies worth'. Indeed, as signalling systems are modernised, there is greater concentration into fewer boxes which are bound to cover areas used by several companies, leading to similar situations.

Response: Railtrack told Mr Clement that management was 'unaware' of any problems and that the control centre was large enough to accommodate the extra people with ease. 'Safety,' she added, 'would always be top priority and in any case normally only two train operators were represented at the centre.' Mr King, however, insisted that 'interlopers' from five operators were represented in the centre.

A BRT technician installs all the private telephone wires to enable the 75 occupants of a modern power signalbox to keep in touch with their individual trains.

59. So You Want the Right Fare for the Journey?

Which? magazine sent researchers to ring up or go to stations where several train operators ran routes between the same destinations to see whether the information provided was impartial.

The report, published in January 1996, made pretty damning reading, and suggested that thousands of passengers were being overcharged for their journeys, or were not offered full information on which to base their journeys.

To take just a few of the *Which?* examples, on the London to Bath route, the researcher asked for the cheapest return to arrive in Bath by 10.30. None out of 22 replies gave South Wales and West's service which cost £22 from Waterloo. This is £31 cheaper than Great Western's £53 fare out of Paddington. Ticket clerks at InterCity West Coast disagreed, some suggesting £53 while others said £45. Researchers for the journey in the opposite direction to arrive in London by the same time fared slightly better with four out of 21 getting the right answer, which was South Wales and West's £30 fare, £23 cheaper than Great Western's £53. Admittedly the service is an hour slower and goes to Waterloo — but then some people will reckon £23 is worth an hour of their time and also many might find Waterloo closer to their ultimate destination in London.

When asking what the cheapest first class return leaving around noon from London to Exeter, the price variation was even greater. Five out of eight times the researchers were told that the fare was £116, a staggering £70.20 more than the cheapest South West Trains option. The £116 fare is Great Western's most expensive first class return per mile, according to *Which?*, and it is the wrong fare even on Great Western as there is a £76.55 first class fare on the relevant train.

Of course the South West Trains Exeter service is slower, but then again handier for people coming from south London or points south of London as it leaves from Waterloo. Not surprisingly, it was only the Waterloo telephone booking office which offered the correct £45.80 ticket. Overall, the answers given for this journey were overpriced by just under £50.

A similar pattern was found on the London to Birmingham route where passengers have a choice of the Chiltern line service to Birmingham Snow Hill and the more widely known InterCity Great Western journey (see also No 31). Chiltern charge £22 while InterCity charge £55 for a journey that takes an hour less. InterCity's offices never offered the cheapest Chiltern fare to any of their eight enquirers, though one sold a Chiltern day return fare for £37. However, two days later that same booking office told the researcher that the cheapest fare available was £55.

Response: British Rail put out a pretty po-faced press release which clearly its own press officers hardly found convincing. It said: 'The *Which?* report is misleading and unrepresentative of the experience of the majority of rail passengers. It concentrates on a handful of routes on which there are alternative travel options which are not typical of the system as a whole.

'There has been a fundamental

change in the way train tickets are sold, from a national range of 55 million fares available by any reasonable route to a wide range of additional fares specific to individual operators. Inevitably, it takes time for staff to familiarise themselves with the new arrangements and with the large number of new fares.

'The *Which?* survey was carried out four months ago, since when the train operating companies have undertaken a huge amount of the training needed. Train operating company managers understand the need to ensure that customers have the impartial information they have every right to expect. That is already widely provided and all will continue to work to ensure that inadvertent exceptions are eliminated.'

Comment: The rail regulator is supposed to ensure that information given by one rail company is entirely impartial. But in a way that is going against the grain of the way that business is conducted. The whole ethos of the rail privatisation drive is to instil private sector disciplines and attitudes into the industry. Employees of private firms are not expected to co-operate with their rivals. People selling Heinz baked beans will hardly suggest that you buy Crosse and Blackwell instead because they are on a cheap offer. Ticket office clerks are employed by the train operating companies and not Railtrack or some other overall body. Therefore, they are bound to favour their own company, even unwittingly as they will simply be much better informed about their own firm's activities than those of their rivals. It is not, therefore, as BR suggests, a matter of more training. It is an endemic problem caused by the very nature of this privatisation and several readers have written in to report similar incidents to those uncovered by *Which?* (see, for example, Nos 13, 21, 31 and 33). And while BR is right to point out that there are not that many journeys on which two alternative routes can be used, one of the initial tenets of privatisation was to boost on-rail competition.

60. So You Want a Local Travelcard for Buses and Trains?

A travelcard enabling people on the south coast to use the local train and bus services without having to buy tickets for every journey is to be scrapped as a result of rail privatisation.

More than 120,000 people in Brighton and the surrounding area currently use the scheme which allows them access to all local public transport. Over £1.5 million in revenue was raised by local bus companies from the travelcard system, which also saves money for intensive users of public transport by offering them a cheaper deal than individual tickets.

After 17 years of co-operation between the local bus companies and British Rail, Network SouthCentral, the region's train company, has announced its intention to withdraw unilaterally from the scheme, claiming it is not cost-effective.

The bus firms say they will not only lose revenue, but as more passengers will have to buy tickets from the drivers of one-person-operated buses, there will be more traffic delays.

In a letter to Brighton Council, Network SouthCentral's business manager, Harinder Dhesi, said: 'Network SouthCentral have made it clear that... the percentage shares offered to us were no longer commercially realistic.' The travelcard will be withdrawn from 1 October 1995 unless Brighton Council can obtain government support.'

The Brighton travelcard was one of the first to be introduced in Britain and its demise suggests that many other similar schemes around the country could be put in jeopardy. Steve Bassam, leader of the Labour-controlled council, said: 'This seems to fly in the face of attempts to develop a coherent local transport strategy which enables people to make the best use of public transport.'

Update: The local Travelcard system collapsed on 1 October 1995 as a result of this dispute. Although existing cardholders could continue to use their tickets, no new ones were being issued. However, as the book went to press Brighton Council was still in negotiations with the rail companies hoping that the Travelcard scheme could be reinstated.

Comment: The future of similar travelcards is likely to be put at risk by privatisation as disputes over revenue appear inevitable. Already, fraud has delayed the privatisation of the London, Tilbury and Southend line in February 1996, caused by the commercial manager of the new management buy-out company — with the unfortunate name of Enterprise Rail — moving tickets between stations to maximise revenue. Tickets sold at Fenchurch Street were allocated on the basis of 78:22 between LTS and London Transport, while those sold at Upminster were allocated on the basis of 52:48. This is because the tickets included a London Transport Travelcard element and it was assumed that people buying tickets at Upminster are more likely to use the Tube because it is on the Underground's District Line than those at Fenchurch Street where there is no tube station. Therefore, this clever chap issued tickets at Fenchurch Street and sold them at Upminster in order to maximise LTS's revenue. In the days when all the railways and LT were run by the public sector, such shenanigans would have been irrelevant. Under privatisation, they are inevitable. And so are disputes about the allocation of revenue which is bound to be to some extent arbitrary, however sophisticated the systems are. One can imagine a privatised LTS immediately embarking on arguments about why they get only around half the revenue at Upminster and so on and on...

61. So There are Too Many People Trying to Use the Trains?

Passengers on the Exmouth to Paignton line in Devon faced fare rises of 56% because a local train company wanted to stifle demand on the section of the line between Teignmouth and Torre. John Silverman found that the weekly child season ticket for his 13-year-old son Steven to travel the seven miles from Teignmouth to Torre station, Torquay, to go to school had risen from £6.35 in January 1995 to £9.90 in May 1995. A letter from South Wales and West said that the price changes were made because of 'an extreme demand situation'. Apparently, 250 people, mainly local students, have been trying to cram on to the 150-seater train which arrives at Torre at 08.33, in time for the children to get to school. The return train at 16.12 has also been very overcrowded.

Mr Silverman said the cost of sending his son to school had gone up from £200 to £300 per year and said: 'We are now considering with other parents hiring a coach to get the children to school.'

The problem was initially caused by the weight restrictions on a road bridge which made the bus journey too circuitous to be economic. Therefore, the buses stopped operating and everyone had to use the trains, causing an 80% increase on the best train for schoolchildren.

The rail company does not have the additional rolling stock to increase the length of the train. Indeed, according to Sean O'Neill, the secretary of the local rail users' committee, the company is so short of trains that 'it has already replaced half the services between Avonmouth and Severn Beach with a bus because the trains were needed on another route'.

South Wales and West were also supposed to have alerted Mr O'Neill's organisation to the increase, but he said: 'There is supposed to be a statutory duty for them to inform us, but the system has not worked since the reorganisation of the railways in 1994.'

The problem, at root, is privatisation. A BR spokesman explained: 'Before the break-up of the railways in April 1994, there was spare rolling stock, but now it is too expensive for operators to keep it.' This is because it all now belongs to the Roscos (see No 55 above) who lease it out at very high rates. A spokesman for South Wales and West reckoned that an extra coach would cost £100,000 per year, with total costs, including fuel and wages, of around £250,000. The extra revenue would have at most been £20,000.

Mike Patterson, of the passengers' watchdog CRUCC, warned that other train companies might follow suit: 'We see this as a negative reaction to a particularly localised overcrowding problem. There could be repercussions elsewhere if other train operating companies follow the same principle.'

Eryl Jones, spokesman for South Wales and West, said that the increase on the Exmouth to Paignton line was unique: 'Overall, our fares went up in May 1995 by just under the inflation rate. And several fares have gone down. We restructured the fares between Teignmouth and Torre in order to suppress demand. We aim to attract sufficient custom to fill the available trains, but not to overcrowd them, in order that customers' value for money aspirations are met.'

He explained that initially after the weight restriction had been imposed on the bridge, the train company had provided a bus in addition to the rail service. But it had only covered one third of its costs and therefore it had been removed.

Response: Sir George Young, the transport secretary, attempted to lay the blame for the ensuing furore on British Rail, saying in Parliament that it was the type of problem rail privatisation was designed to solve. He also claimed that such high increases could not happen because of the fares cap introduced by the franchising director, Roger Salmon, which will limit some fares to the rate of inflation for three years from January 1996 and inflation minus one per cent thereafter.

Update: Eryl Jones updated the situation in February 1996. He said that there was no question of providing extra rolling stock because of the cost. But as a result of the fuss, local schoolchildren had been offered a discount, a weekly season of £6.70 rather than £9.90 if they used the early train which gets into Torre at 07.50. The trouble is it means they have to hang around in the school for an extra 40min. And, in response to the fuss, the price of the Teignmouth to Torre weekly season has been cut by 10% to £8.90 for children.

Interestingly, the even more famous incident involving trains to Sevenoaks raised the same issue. Passengers from Sevenoaks were being forced to pay more to travel to Tonbridge than High Brooms, which is one stop beyond Tonbridge on the line. And if they bought a ticket to High Brooms and got off at Tonbridge, they faced a penalty fare of £10.

South Eastern, the local train company, justified the fares in various ways. It argued that Tonbridge was part of the more expensive suburban London area and that was why it was £2.15 return for children to go from Sevenoaks to Tonbridge, but only £1.65 to High Brooms. But the more interesting explanation came later from South Eastern's press spokesman, Chris Dyson, who told the local *Sevenoaks Chronicle* in January 1996 that 'it may seem unfair but we have to control excessive demand between Sevenoaks and Tonbridge with higher fares. High Brooms is a rural station with fewer users, even in the peak period, so we encourage more people to travel there instead.' John Swift, the rail regulator, ordered South Eastern to stop charging the extra amount while he carried out an investigation into the situation.

Comment: Sir George is being a trifle optimistic. As the item shows, it is the high cost at the margin of introducing trains which will lead to such situations. In other words, far from boosting the number of trains, privatisation is likely to lead to a number of services stagnating. And as Labour's spokesman, Michael Meacher, immediately pointed out in the ensuing debate: 'Long term season tickets are not included in the fares cap and in any case it is the overall basket of fares that will be controlled and not individual ones.' Moreover, only 30% of fares are actually covered by the capping arrangement.

TRAIN TICKETS

TICKET HOLDERS! WHY WAIT ON A COLD PLATFORM FOR UP TO 20 MINS? THE M1 ACCESS ROUTE IS ONLY 10 MINS FROM THE STATION CAR PARK

62. So That's Why the Trains are Going Bumpety Bump (Part 2)

Engineers working for Network SouthCentral, which runs most of the services out of Victoria, suddenly discovered in the spring of 1995 that the wheels of their 250 trains were wearing out much more quickly than normal, around 10 times faster than the usual rate. The problem began to have a real impact on the timetable as trains had to be taken out of service for repair.

While cancellations were kept to a minimum, a lot of trains had to be run at half their normal length causing inconvenience and delays. The management team of Network SouthCentral was tearing its hair out to discover what had happened.

By chance, the engineers discovered the problem. It was caused by the failure of Railtrack to ensure that the curves on rails were being greased properly. To prevent flanges on train wheels being worn down, curves on rails are fitted with grease guns which are operated automatically by the trains going over them. However, for several weeks, it appears that large numbers of these grease guns were not being replenished with lubricant due to an administrative error. The men charged with the job had been made redundant and no one had thought to replace them.

NSC said that not only did it lose a considerable amount of passenger revenue, but also the repairs to the trains were very expensive. Graham Eccles, the director of NSC, said: 'Already in south London a lot of our trains are full and having four carriages instead of eight meant a lot of people

Oil's well that ends well!

couldn't get on the first train or they travelled in unsatisfactory conditions. We have no idea how much revenue we lost because people found our trains too uncomfortable and crowded and went back to using their cars.' He said that new wheels cost around £45–£50,000 for a train set and while they can sometimes reprofile them at a cost of £15,000, that can only be done a limited number of times.

It was the separation of Railtrack from British Rail in preparation for privatisation which led to the problem. When Railtrack launched an investigation into the error, its managers blamed the South Western Infrastructure Management Unit, its contractor, which is responsible for maintenance of NSC's lines. SWIMU is also being prepared for privatisation, but is still owned by British Rail. One Railtrack manager likened the organisation's position to being the meat in the sandwich between two different parts of BR, since NSC is still part of BR.

Update: Network SouthCentral had threatened to sue Railtrack over the problem as the damage to the wheels and loss of revenue were estimated to be £1.2 million, but in the end an amicable out of court agreement was reached. Privately, the management told the 'Mad' column that if both organisations had been privatised, rather than still both being in the public sector, then legal action would have been inevitable.

After the grease gun problem was discovered, the rates of wheel wear returned to normal immediately.

Railtrack's solution for avoiding the necessity of rail maintenance — remove the track completely!

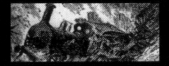

63. So You Want to Use the Fire Extinguisher?

Railworkers put out a trackside fire with mud because they had been banned from using a fire extinguisher as it belonged to a different rail company. The incident, on 27 March 1995, involved a small fire by the track at Beckenham Junction in Kent. It was recorded in a Railtrack log, later leaked by the Labour Party, which said that the fire was 'extinguished by TOU (train operating unit, which was South Eastern) emergency staff by using mud'. Although there was an available fire extinguisher at the station belonging to South Eastern, a notice at the station warned them that using fire extinguishers on Railtrack equipment could result in 'disciplinary action'.

A spokesman for South Eastern accepted that the incident had occurred, but said that the notice was unauthorised and has subsequently been taken down. There would be no recurrence of the incident, he said.

Railtrack said the train operating company managers had put up the notice because they had probably wanted to ensure that the extinguisher was still available for use on train fires. He said: 'This was a mistake. All extinguishers are available for use throughout the railway. It was a local misunderstanding and the notice conveyed the wrong message.'

'Life would be a damn sight easier if we had access to ordinary fire extinguishers ....'

Andrew Bennett frequently travels from Darlington to Exeter on InterCity Cross Country trains and likes to treat himself to a bit of luxury on the long journey by paying the £5 supplement which allows him to sit in the first class compartment.

In late January 1996, he was on the train when the 'senior conductor' asked him to pay the supplement and told him it would be £6. Asked why the price had gone up from £5, the guard said that this was the amount charged on InterCity East Coast and that he was an East Coast employee, rather than a Cross Country one.

Mr Bennett challenged this, pointing out that he was on a Cross Country route, in a Cross Country train, on Railtrack lines and that the journey therefore had nothing to do with East Coast. Mr Bennett, £1 richer as a result of his understandable obstinacy, was later told by a Cross Country 'senior conductor' that he had 'done well to get away with £5 from an East Coast man'. In recent weeks, the Cross Country man explained, he had encountered many problems when he had charged the usual £5 supplement to passengers, because others sitting nearby had been charged £6. This applied to all those who had boarded the train between Newcastle and Doncaster when it was under the charge of an East Coast conductor.

Mr Bennett comments: '£1 is a small and probably insignificant difference, but my experience does raise the issue of which parts of the new service 'belong' to whom, and who takes precedence in levying charges.'

Response/Update: Another likely victory for the 'Mad' column. When this was pointed out to InterCity East Coast, the company's spokesman, Laurie Holland, said: 'Of course this is an error. When our staff are working on Cross Country's trains, they should charge Cross Country's fares. We will instruct our staff accordingly.'

'Yes, I work for Thames Trains. The information you got on the train from Exeter would have come from Great Western. Information at stations? You could have got that from virtually anybody. Who caused the delay? Well, the track's owned by Railtrack. The maintenance was being undertaken by British Rail Infrastructure Services. The failed passenger train was operated by Regional Railways but owned by one of the leasing companies. You want to complain? Well, all I can suggest is that you write to the Secretary of State for Transport; after all, it is the government's madcap scheme that lies at the root of all this!'